T0373663

Border security in the Balkans: Europe's gatekeepers

Alice Hills

ADELPHI PAPER 371

Routledge
Taylor & Francis Group

LONDON AND NEW YORK

First published 2004 by Oxford University Press for the International
Institute for Strategic Studies, Arundel House, 13-15 Arundel Street,
Temple Place, London, WC2R 3DX

This reprint published by Routledge
2 Park Square, Milton Park, Abingdon, Oxon, OX14 4RN
For The International Institute for Strategic Studies
Arundel House, 13-15 Arundel Street, Temple Place, London, WC2R 3DX
www.iiss.org

Simultaneously published in the USA and Canada
by Routledge
270 Madison Ave., New York, NY 10016

Transferred to Digital Printing 2009

Routledge is an imprint of the Taylor & Francis Group

© 2004 The International Institute for Strategic Studies

Director John Chipman
Editor Tim Huxley
Copy Editor David Ucko
Production Simon Nevitt

British Library Cataloguing in Publication data
A catalogue record for this book is available from the British Library

Library of Congress Cataloguing in Publication data

ISBN 0-415-37588-6

Publisher's Note
The publisher has gone to great lengths to ensure the quality of this
reprint but points out that some imperfections in the original may be
apparent.

Contents

Glossary

ANA	Albanian National Army
ANP	Albanian National Police
ARM	Army of the Republic of Macedonia
BCS	Border Crossing Sector
BiH	Bosnia Herzegovina
BSD	Border Service Directorate
CARDS	Community Assistance for Reconstruction, Development and Stabilisation
CIREFI	Centre for Information, Discussion and Exchange on the Crossing of Frontiers and Immigration
EAR	European Agency for Reconstruction
EC	European Commission
EU	European Union
EUPM	European Union Police Mission
EUROPOL	European Police Office
IBM	Integrated Border Management
IBPC	International Border Police Conference
ICAO FAL-Panel	International Civil Aviation Organisation, Facilitation Division
ICMPD	International Centre for Migration Policy Development
ICITAP	International Criminal Investigative Training Assistance Programme
INTERPOL	International Criminal Police Organisation
IOM	International Organisation for Migration
IPTF	International Police Task Force
JHA	Justice and Home Affairs
KFOR	NATO's Kosovo Force
MARRI	Migration, Asylum, Regional Return Initiative
MoI	Ministry of the Interior
OSCE	Organisation for Security and Cooperation in Europe
PHARE	Poland and Hungary Assistance for the Restructuring of the Economy
SAA	Stabilisation and Association Agreement
SAp	Stabilisation and Association process
SBS	State Border Service
SFOR	Stabilisation Force in Bosnia and Herzegovina
SWOT	Strengths, Weaknesses, Opportunities and Threats
UNHCR	United Nations High Commissioner for Refugees
UNMIBH	United Nations Mission in Bosnia Herzegovina
UNMIK	United Nations Interim Administration Mission in Kosovo
USAID	United States Agency for International Development

Introduction

Borders dominate the security agenda in South-east Europe. Demarcation is controversial, security has yet to be de-territorialised, and the Balkans are a region of traditional smuggling routes, organised crime and corruption. Current border control is ineffective.

A dramatic increase in uncontrolled migration and illegal trafficking brought these issues to the fore in 1999, when improving the management of South-east Europe's porous borders became a priority for the EU. It was clear that without international pressure for reform, the region's under-resourced, inexperienced and inadequately trained border guards would not challenge the gangs trafficking migrants and drugs, mostly intended for the EU. At its Zagreb summit of November 2000, the EU formally identified the need to develop effective border management in the region, and for existing border systems to adopt its functional standards. The term 'border management' refers to the processes and procedures associated with border checks, which take place at authorised crossing points, and 'border surveillance', which is carried out on the so-called green (that is, land) borders between these authorised crossing points.

Border security represents the empirical manifestation of a state's adaptation to its external environment. Nonetheless, functional border security remains generally neglected by the wider security community. Borders are discussed in terms of EU expansion, identity politics, visa regimes, illegal trafficking, and uncontrolled migration, rather than guarding, with the result that a topic of potentially strategic significance is only partially understood.[1]

This paper redresses the balance. Its purpose is to examine the development of border management in South-east Europe, the location of many security issues, and its implications for Europe's immediate future. 'South-east Europe' is the preferred term here because it emphasises the relevance to the EU of developments in countries such as Bosnia Herzegovina (BiH) and Macedonia. Many commentators use it interchangeably with the EU term 'western Balkans', which has been in common use since 1999; the difference is primarily one of political emphasis. More importantly, the paper assesses the changing nature, form and location of state responses in terms of the agents managing borders: border guards. The term 'border guards' is often used interchangably with 'border police', but the former is prefered here. Border control is about law enforcement as well as the protection of borders, and most states in the EU's sphere of influence categorise their guards as police, but, the term 'guards' emphasises that border guards are ideally independent and specialist multipurpose police, subordinated to the ministry of the interior but not forming part of the national police force.[2]

This paper examines the assumptions and principles underpinning contemporary explanations of guarding and the social realities that determine its effectiveness, basing its approach on the premise that current border-security developments result from a combination of political, ideological, functional and cultural variables. The dynamics of guarding in South-eastern Europe are shaped by political imperatives (primarily those of the EU and national elites), perceived security challenges (uncontrolled migration and organised crime), and socio-economic challenges (corruption, poverty, and under-development). Trends in formal and informal regulation are identified, as are the strategic options available to each state and issues of convergence and divergence in practice between states. The result is a more nuanced understanding of contemporary security issues in South-east Europe.

A subsidiary concern centres on the extent to which today's broad definition of security can provide a sound basis for understanding border security. Tensions between conventional and 'new-security' threats (which are not manageable by military force alone), and between military and police powers, are explicit in the region's border management. Theoretical questions of how to secure, by whom, against whom, to what end, and by what means and methods represent practical problems for border managers. Effective border security requires the reassertion of the state's coercive authority and increasingly, the promotion of the EU's vision of political order and security-sector reform. The control, filtering and exclusion of individuals or groups must be balanced by the facilitation of legitimate traffic and better communication between guards and travellers. By investigating such issues, insight can be gained into the distinctive ways of managing an important aspect of European security.

Border security matters, then, for political, practical, and theoretical reasons. Border guards operate at the intersection of a number of topical concerns, where many security problems present themselves with particular intensity. They manage the interface of external and internal security, military and police powers, conventional and new-security threats, and old and new Europe. Trends in border management in South-east Europe also offer insight into the creation of institutions thought necessary for viable statehood and for capacity-building more generally. They are indicative of the role of borders in the post-Cold-War world, and the extent to which effective management of trans-border challenges requires the integration of international, regional, national and functional interests.

Assessing change

This paper's key task is to assess the changing nature of state responses to insecurity in South-east Europe's border regions.

The answer offered is threefold. Many recent developments in regional border management are explicable in terms of the burden-shifting logic informing EU policy-making, whereby the costs of common initiatives (concerning the processing of illegal immigrants, for example) are shifted to transit countries. The extent to which politically-motivated changes in the rationale or meaning of border security are prioritised over the transformation of guarding structures is, however, difficult to assess: guarding reflects a mix of political, ideological, cultural and functional variables. Even so, explanations that neglect functional border management can only provide a partial basis for understanding security in the region.

This conclusion is reached in four stages. Chapter 1 introduces the assumptions and principles underpinning contemporary border management. It discusses the major characteristics, variables and problems of border policing in the region, the EU's influential model of integrated border management (IBM), and the extent to which border security transcends traditional security preoccupations. The strategic options available to the governments of the region are addressed in Chapters 2 and 3, which show how state actors and agencies understand the predicament of regional insecurity, and why they invent strategies that allow them to accommodate, evade or subvert unavoidable political pressures. In particular, Chapter 2 explores the strategies, principles, options, and problems confronting new or reformed systems, and the challenges associated with transferring democratic standards of border management between states for border policing in BiH and Slovenia. BiH is introduced first because it is a European protectorate, which makes explicit the assumptions underpinning its system, while Slovenia's border security is now harmonised with that of the EU. Older, more entrenched problems are analysed in Chapter 3, which compares border security in the Former Yugoslav Republic of Macedonia (hereafter Macedonia) and Albania, where paramilitary challenges and social realities subvert political proposals for EU styles of border management. Each chapter addresses three specific questions: What are the available strategic options? What significant features and assumptions are identifiable? How should recent developments be assessed?[3]

Of the four countries examined, the inclusion of Slovenia is the most questionable. Slovenia is undoubtedly part of South-east Europe geographically, but for historical, political and economic reasons it does not regard itself as part of the Balkans. Neither does the EU, which categorises the western Balkans as comprising Albania, BiH, Croatia, Macedonia, and Serbia and Montenegro. Its inclusion does, however, provide an informative success-story for the wider region.

The examples used illustrate four distinct aspects of border-security systems:

- Border management as state-formation (BiH)
- Capacity-building in response to political objectives (Slovenia)
- Adaptive functional imperatives (Macedonia)
- The impact of socio-economic conditions (Albania)

The approach provides a spectrum of examples, ranging from border systems that are harmonised with EU standards to those that barely function. It acknowledges the importance of regional dynamics but avoids the possibility of producing too narrow and specific an explanation. Based on this approach, Chapter 4 identifies common patterns of development, and the shared regional assumptions underpinning contemporary explanations and practice. It gauges the extent to which a consensual European approach to border security is developing, before concluding that the ability of international organisations to create effective and efficient systems of border management is uncertain, as the border regions in the Balkans remain potentially subversive.

Chapter 1

Assumptions, principles and strategy

Many security threats are present on South-east Europe's borders. The risk of conflict has lessened since the surrender of Slobodan Milosevic in 2001 but not disappeared; political and ethnic discontents focus on disputed borders; and criminal gangs and illegal migrants cross them.

Caches of arms and ammunition are hidden along Albania's northern borders, which are isolated by bad roads, mountains and rural poverty, while attempts by Macedonia's security forces to clamp down on the gangs running smuggling routes between Macedonia and Serbia increase political tensions in Kosovo and Serbia and Montenegro. Disputes regarding the location of boundaries or border crossings are frequently used to obstruct political settlements. Macedonia, for example, faces external challenges resulting from the uncertain status of Kosovo and the refusal of neighbouring states to recognise Macedonia's own identity. In April 2003, Macedonian Prime Minister Branko Crvenkovski argued that attempts to change borders or exchange populations are a 'direct call for ethnic war'; his Defence Minister Vlado Buckovski stated flatly on 25 December 2003 that the resolution of Kosovo's final political status would depend on the satisfactory delineation of Macedonia's borders.[1] Significantly, the death of President Boris Trajkovski of Macedonia in a plane crash in a heavily land-mined mountainous area on the border between BiH and Croatia on 26 February 2004 was immediately perceived as a potential threat to national security, resulting in heightened security along Macedonia's borders and at key state and army institutions. More recently, the November 2004 referendum on the redrawing of municipal boundaries is likely to result in months of acrimonious wrangling and increased tensions, as the majority of Macedonians believe that the real aim of the ethnic Albanians (who represent one-quarter of the population of two million) is to partition the country as a first step towards creating a Greater Albania.

Regional politics, meanwhile, are overshadowed by allegations of illegal trafficking. Criminal networks are adept at exploiting the foibles or greed of politicians, businessmen and security officers, and corruption is endemic, affecting most of the organisations involved in border security.[2] The smuggling of illegal migrants, drugs, cigarettes, cars and weapons, together with the trafficking of women and, to a lesser extent, children affect all countries in the region. Negligence on the part of border guards remains a major obstacle to effective border control. The implications for the EU are acute, given that the Balkans are the main gateway for illegal drugs, goods and migrants into Western Europe. To quantify the problem accurately is impossible, but several thousand illegal migrants probably pass through countries such as BiH each month. The situation has improved since 2000, when the International Organisation for Migration (IOM) estimated that more than 50,000 illegal migrants passed through BiH on their way to the EU, but it remains serious.[3] Not surprisingly, effective border security is one of the EU's strategic priorities for the region.

Border guarding

Border guards control migration, demonstrate sovereignty, and often represent an important source of state budgetary income, but until recently their role was seen as being of technical interest only. At best, guarding was understood as an occupation in which narrowly-defined skills were acquired through experience. At worst, guards were seen as the poor relations of police forces, usually despised in the region. Police studies neglected guards, as did the literature on border management, which focused largely on the changing nature of borders, the need for international cooperation, apprehensions, measures to combat trafficking, and the means for making border control more effective.[4]

This condition of neglect is changing as a result of reconstruction and security-sector reform programmes implemented in the aftermath of the Balkan wars, international concern regarding increasing levels of transnational crime and illegal migration, and the EU's strategic agenda for the EU and European border security. In particular, crime and uncontrolled migration threaten the EU's goal of regional integration, which is based on a series of inclusionary and exclusionary policies whose enforcement depends on effective border management. The promotion of effective and politically acceptable styles of guarding in the states bordering the EU is consequently significant, not least because it marks a shift in interest by the international community from border delineation to border management.

Delineation remains important and necessary: the break-up of former Yugoslavia created more than 5,000 kilometres of new international borders, many of which remain the focus of major security and social problems. Not only are border regions notoriously poor and neglected by their governments, but many borders are also unmarked and challenged by secessionist minorities. Decades of shifting borders have resulted in bitter controversies regarding, for example, the rights of ethnic Albanians in Macedonia and Serbia. Nationalist parties flourish in such circumstances; all three communities in BiH have their own parties, while pan-Albanianism is strong across much of the region.[5]

Delineation is for these reasons controversial; it often highlights seemingly intractable conflicts and all too often represents a potential flashpoint. Delineation between Serbia and Kosovo, for example, would symbolise the final break-up of the old Balkans system, while in other cases – notably Macedonia – it might destroy any lingering illusion of a homogeneous, centralised, or ethnically-mixed nation-state. Whereas any division of BiH would require international boundaries to be changed, delineation in Kosovo would involve upgrading, rather than changing, current boundaries or borders from those of a province to those of a state.

Given such problems, it is not surprising that interest within the EU and the Organisation for Security and Cooperation in Europe (OSCE) has shifted in the last three or four years to the more practical and accessible problems of border management. The EU increasingly focuses on the pragmatic themes of integration, cooperation, liaison, reliability and commonality, all of which seem specifically designed to provide comprehensive and politically uncontroversial solutions to a raft of local, national and regional security problems. For example, in its country strategy paper for BiH for the period 2002–06, the European Commission (EC) specifically notes the need for the EU and BiH to develop a 'comprehensive solution' to the known (and accessible) problems of organised crime and corruption, trafficking and illegal migration.[6] For the EC, better border management will involve improving border crossings, strengthening national institutions and procedures, developing the capabilities and infrastructure of border agencies, and increasing interagency cooperation. It will also demarcate borders. Border guards are the functional agents performing the checks, liaison and crime fighting on which such objectives depend.

Border guarding tends to be subsumed under policing, but the role played by guards and the nature of their tasks are more significant than this implies. On the one hand, most guards are technically police, even if some are really interior troops. Their tasks range from customs duties to military-style border patrols, though international-reform programmes invariably advocate an independent and specialised role for guards that emphasises policing responsibilities at the expense of combat-related capabilities. Furthermore, managing human trafficking and migration is essentially a policing activity: responding to the smuggling of aliens involves border guards working with aliens' police, criminal police, other government agencies, and with non-governmental organisations (NGOs) and international organisations. On the other hand, guards need some paramilitary capacity in order to confront armed gangs in sparsely populated border zones. Indeed, the operational demands of managing land borders ensure that even police-oriented guards require a rapid-reaction response underpinned by military-style discipline. As a result, they often represent a multifunctional enforcement authority.

In this way, border guards occupy a significant space on the spectrum of security forces. They exercise both police and military functions and roles that involve close working relationships (and rivalries) with police and military forces, not least because the geographic border is also the psychological and professional border between police and military roles and duties. They operate at the boundaries of internal and external security, and of national and regional concerns. In South-east Europe, they also represent the extensive reconstruction that the international community has promoted, financed and directed in preparation for the region's integration into the EU's sphere of influence. Their broader role is emphasised by the perceived linkage between border management and the EU's expanded security concerns regarding organised crime, uncontrolled migration, and corruption. Guarding is also linked to customs control and the facilitation of trade, while the functional centrality of document control and visa regimes means that border management is relevant to migration control and anti-terrorist campaigns.

The precise role played by the region's border guards varies according to context, but their formal purpose is to provide a public security mission that is nowadays intended to prevent illegal entry and trafficking, repatriate foreigners who have illegally entered the state, admit foreigners when appropriate, and provide assistance to other authorities in their capacity as a specialised but multipurpose police force. Typically, they monitor and detect crime in border regions; this includes illegal trafficking, property offences (often involving stolen vehicles), weapons crimes, and the use of forged or false documents. Many also provide border protection, controlling cross-border traffic at official crossing points, in border areas, along known migration routes and in sections between border-crossing points on land or maritime and river borders (green or blue borders, respectively). They also exercise a filter effect, integrating the various national and international elements needed for local, national and, increasingly, regional security. This means that even the most ineffective national authorities are expected to cooperate with the Schengen authorities and international organisations such as EUROPOL, the Budapest-based International Border Police Conference (IBPC), the EU's Centre for Information, Discussion and Exchange on the Crossing of Frontiers and Immigration (CIREFI), and the International Civil Aviation Organisation, Facilitation Division (ICAO FAL-Panel), as well as networks of border-liaison officers.

Such international agencies are important for a variety of reasons. In particular, their number emphasises that guarding cannot be a purely functional matter, least of all in the EU's sphere of influence, because borders continue to play a central symbolic role in European politics. Indeed, Peter Andreas' argument that the intensification of policing on the EU's borders has less to do with deterring illegal trafficking and migration than 'recrafting the image of the border and symbolically reaffirming the state's territorial authority' is pertinent for the impact of the EU on regional border management.[7]

Schengen's security space

The attention focused on border management (as opposed to the delineation of borders) reflects two linked trends, which shape both the EU and South-eastern Europe's understanding of the purpose of state authority on the border. The first is that effective border control is of direct concern to the EU, while the second follows from the ambition of the region's states to be recognised as part of modern Europe, or, better still, as EU members.

There are two distinct yet related reasons why improving border management is of vital interest to the EU: it plays a central role in EU enlargement and, more generally, it allays Western Europe's security fears regarding organised crime.

Enlargement

The EU's security strategy has traditionally involved the creation of a hard external border for the Union, which is based on Schengen procedural standards and difficult to breach. This is achieved in parallel with the dismantling of internal borders. A Justice and Home Affairs (JHA) programme is used to create an area of 'freedom, justice and security' within an open EU, and incorporates practices ranging from common visa policies and border procedures to judicial cooperation designed to fight organised crime and terrorism. External border checks replace those previously conducted at common borders, a common definition of the rules for crossing external borders is used, and the rules regarding conditions of entry and visas for short stays are harmonised. The various national administrations in member states coordinate their border-surveillance procedures by such means as political guidance, liaison officers and staff training.

The key point of the system is that the common external border is policed by nationally-based guards employing a rigorous system of checks and filters that requires a significant administrative and cooperative capacity on the part of the guards concerned. Effective border management depends on trust, predictability and liaison as well as institutional integration. However, the scale of the most recent enlargement programme in May 2004 (the accession candidates were the Cyprus, Czech Republic, Hungary, Malta, Poland, Slovakia, Slovenia, and the three Baltic republics) has the potential to challenge this arrangement. Accession has never meant automatic inclusion in the Schengen area of borderless movement, but the proximity of states such as Slovenia and Hungary to fragile and notoriously corrupt neighbours such as Albania and Ukraine could potentially compromise the policing of the EU's external borders. In particular, the recent round of enlargement not only gives the EU an external border with the Balkans in the form of the southern borders of Slovenia and Hungary (though neither will join the Schengen zone until 2007), but the new member states also lie alongside countries that are unlikely candidates for membership and where organised crime is rife.

The EU's approach to such security problems involves integration programmes built on a combination of development assistance, power projection, and conventional border security. Furthermore, the EU accepts that dealing with the economic and political reconstruction of the Balkans is its responsibility, not Washington's: for the US, the Balkans are now a strategic backwater. The EU has repeatedly stated that its objective is the 'fullest possible integration of the countries of the Western Balkans into the political and economic mainstream of Europe'.[8] The European Council confirmed this in Feira in June 2000, for instance, as did the Copenhagen European Council in December 2002. The Brussels European Council of March 2003 reaffirmed that 'the future of the Western Balkans [lies] within the EU' and that 'the preparation of the countries of the Western Balkans for integration into European structures is a major priority ... The unification of Europe will not be complete until these countries join the European Union'.[9]

South-east Europe has welcomed this approach. The lure or prospect of EU membership has undoubtedly influenced the policies for border management developed in the region, and most countries hold some form of dialogue with the EU. Many people in the Balkans wish for closer relations because 'we are European', while others see the EU as a rich or benign empire that can bring prosperity and stability, and an escape from the poverty and corruption commonly attributed to the region's politicians.

As a result of such trends, the EU has been able to address the security dilemmas of enlargement and new non-state threats by developing a range of cooperation goals and arrangements with non-members in what is known as the external dimension of EU cooperation in JHA.[10] These measures are usually expressed in terms of traditional policy tools, such as cooperation between relevant border-security forces, or the provision of expert assistance or training packages. The external dimension includes financial inducements and preventive measures, such as development assistance, that are designed to promote cooperation and a degree of procedural predictability, and, more importantly, keep problems (such as uncontrolled migrants or refugees) away from the EU's area of borderless travel. The security burden is either shared or shifted, depending on case specifics.[11]

This approach has worked relatively well so far, but its future is uncertain; a single external border is, after all, only as strong as its weakest link. For this reason, the social and political realities of the states on the EU's border matter – and the boundaries between politics, the security forces, business and organised crime are blurred in most of South-east Europe.

Europe's security fears

The significance of the EU border strategy for the Balkans is emphasised by the three main security threats feared by the EU: uncontrolled migration, the trafficking of illegal drugs, and terrorism. These three issues are often difficult to disentangle, let alone manage. Uncontrolled migration offers profitable business opportunities to organised crime, which often supports terrorism, while the links between politics and organised crime in Albania, for instance, are so tight that rooting out crime in Kosovo carries significant potential political and security risks for Macedonia as well as Serbia, both of which have their own problems in this area. The prioritisation of the three security challenges varies according to circumstances and viewpoints, but border security through patrols and checks is generally thought to represent an important line of defence against all three.

Terrorism

The threat of terrorism is in the context of the Balkans overshadowed by the fear of uncontrolled migration and smuggling. This is not to say that terrorism is not a major strategic priority for the EU. Indeed, the inadequacy of the EU's traditional forms of security cooperation was highlighted by the suicide hijackings of 11 September 2001, as four of the terrorists responsible were based in Germany. In 2002, the EU adopted a new framework decision to focus its anti-terrorism operations and, in the same vein, the EC formally stated in December 2003 that 'the fight against terrorism is one of the highest priorities of the European Union'.[12] Additional counter-terrorism measures were announced at an EU summit in the aftermath of the Madrid bombings in March 2004, and in April, a debate over the European Parliament's draft report on human rights condemned terrorism as one of the most serious threats facing the international community, arguing that fighting terrorism is now the EU's highest priority.

These statements are general, rather than focused on specific Balkans countries. Nonetheless, they are undoubtedly influenced by the known or suspected opportunities offered to terrorists by the Balkans, where security agencies are under-resourced and levels of surveillance lower than in the EU and central Europe. What is more, Islamist groups have taken root in the Balkans. In BiH, for example, Islamic radicals have long been suspected of seeking to introduce their particular style of politics, while the line between terrorism and insurgency in Macedonia and Kosovo is sometimes a fine one.

Even so, neither Macedonia nor Kosovo has seen a large-scale influx of foreign fighters and the evidence for the existence of domestic terrorist organisations in the region is contentious. There are, however, many Russian mafia gangs, which are suspected of trading or cooperating with al-Qaeda supporters. Terrorists may use the Balkans as a means to gain weapons or resources, but one reason why they do so must be the willingness of the Russian mafias in the region to do business; established smuggling routes can often accommodate weapons smuggling as easily as drugs or people. Ultimately, it is difficult to distinguish between terrorism and crime. Indeed, the EU's new anti-terrorist framework of 2002 defined terrorism as a serious form of crime that is to be prevented and combated by closer cooperation between police forces (including border guards), customs authorities and other competent authorities. Significantly, many of the EU measures announced in March 2004 deal with surveillance or crime in general, rather than terrorism as such.

The EU's insistence on border security as a matter for specialist police reinforces the perception that border control should at the very least filter or manage the documentation that terrorists use. However, it is not always easy to distinguish between terrorism, crime and internal politics. Politicians in the Balkans have for instance been known to exploit the label 'terrorism' for domestic political purposes. One notorious case occurred in 2002, when, in an attempt to improve Macedonia's standing in the EU and Washington (and justify future actions against Albanian groups in the country), government officials and police officers in Macedonia shot a group of illegal Pakistani immigrants on the border with Bulgaria, and planted their bodies (dressed in the uniforms of Albanian insurgents and equipped with weapons and the Koran) on the border with Kosovo.[13] In effect, the Macedonians claimed that they too were contributing to the War on Terror.

Uncontrolled migration

There is less ambiguity about the threat presented by uncontrolled migrants transiting through the Balkans into EU member states: the associated fear arguably drives the EU's border-security strategy for the region. Conflict in the early and mid-1990s caused a sharp rise in the number of refugees entering the EU, but the late 1990s saw another sharp rise in the number of economic migrants and refugees entering member states via the Balkans, this time from Afghanistan, China, the Indian sub-continent, Iran and Africa. As far as political, professional, and popular opinion was concerned, migrants became a threat closely linked to organised crime and terrorism. Such fears were often based on incontrovertible facts. Take the case of Albania, a major base for organised crime and a transit point on several established overland smuggling routes leading from all its neighbouring countries, with flows coming from Greece and Macedonia, and from Kosovo, southern Serbia and Montenegro. Albania's inadequately policed coast is, at its narrowest point, only 41km across the Adriatic from Italy. Moreover, though Albania has a comprehensive legislative framework for dealing with migration and asylum claimants that is in line with internationally recognised standards, it chooses not to implement or enforce the relevant provisions. It is impossible to say how many illegal migrants travel through Albania each year, but in 2001 the EC's Country Strategy team for Albania estimated that at least 36,000 persons transited Albania while attempting to migrate to the EU.[14]

Not surprisingly, the EU's primary objectives for Albania for 2002–06 focus on fighting the organised crime, fraud and corruption associated with trafficking. These objectives include establishing higher levels of security on Albania's international borders so as to 'diminish cross border crime and illegal migration'.[15] In the meantime, the smuggling of illegal migrants remains one of the most profitable and low-risk activities for organised-crime groups in Albania and South-east Europe generally. These gangs do not need special equipment or established distribution networks, and illegal migrants are willing to pay substantial sums of money in advance.

Regardless of whether or not the EU's fears regarding uncontrolled migration are realistic, conventional border-control policies often appeared inadequate even before EU enlargement in 2004. It was clear by the late 1990s that incompetent or ineffective border security on the EU's periphery had the potential to undermine the EU's political project and its attempts to stabilise countries such as BiH and Macedonia, to say nothing of Albania and its eastern neighbours. In the 1990s – in the aftermath of the Balkan wars – the EU was primarily concerned with restoring security and stability in the western Balkans, but this had changed by 2000, when it was evident that new forms of cooperation were required if the EU's periphery was to be policed effectively, appropriately, and in accordance with both Schengen's standards and liberal democratic ideals. In reality, the balance between cooperation and control varied according to context, and the extent of EU influence.

However, the EU's own approach to immigration and asylum policies lacked transparency and was highly control-oriented. In the circumstances, the 'export of [Schengen's] control instruments to countries outside the EU can be seen as a logical extension' of the EU's existing approach.[16] As Boswell notes:

> *It took no great leap of the imagination to extend already established forms of EU or Schengen transnational cooperation to additional countries, whether in the form of so-called "pre-frontier control", or capacity building of migration management and asylum systems in transit countries, or the deployment of EU police to combat migrant trafficking in the western Balkans.*[17]

Nor, it might be added, did it require much imagination to send German or French experts to advise the region's existing or fledgling border systems. The countries concerned were either encouraged or (in the case of candidate countries) obliged to apply EU standards of migration control, and cooperation usually meant the acceptance of EU advice and support.

This approach was legitimised by appeals to security threats, member states' concerns, and international human-rights legislation. It was reinforced by the international consensus that the region's corrupt and repressive security forces must be reformed. In December 2002, for instance, the EC warned the leaders of the western Balkans that the region would be left behind the rest of Europe if it failed to strengthen its administrative and judicial capacity; the linkage between corruption and human trafficking was explicitly recognised. The task of exporting EU standards was made easier by the United States' insistence on the creation of a border service in BiH, and by requests from the governments of, for example, Slovenia and Serbia that they receive international technical assistance in developing national strategies for border security. In this way, the EU presented its standards of border security as mutually beneficial forms of partnership.

The EU has yet to define precisely what forms of cooperation and types of preventive policies can best achieve its policy objectives but, in the meantime, engaging transit countries in functionally based programmes works relatively well. Migration has in this way become part of the relationships between the EU and its neighbours.[18] It has also become linked to EU enlargement and to the EU's efforts to combat terrorism. The admission of ten new countries in 2004, for example, means that states such as Albania and BiH, which hold important transit routes for migrants from Asia to the EU, play an increasingly important role in the EU's defences, as do Kosovo and Romania. Meanwhile, the intractability of the problem means that countries such as Italy can present their own migration problems (and their seeming inability to control the activities of Albanian traffickers) as a matter of European security.

Organised crime

More importantly, threats of uncontrolled migration and terrorism bring to the fore the role played by organised crime in the region. There are three reasons why organised crime represents the most fundamental and significant security fear for the EU: is tightly linked to the nature of the societies that permit or tolerate it; it is the enabler that facilitates the transfer of illegal goods and people to the EU's member states; and it is a diverse phenomenon that cannot be managed by conventional European security means.

The Balkans have long been notorious for the ruthlessness and effectiveness of their organised crime and for the high-level protection many criminals enjoy, yet organised crime remains ill-defined and its capabilities are not necessarily well-understood by EU enforcement agencies. The linkage between traffickers and the society in which they operate, for example, is usually inaccessible to outside agents; thus Albanian-organised crime in Kosovo follows the clan structures and norms of society there and in northern Albania, and is impenetrable to Macedonian guards. This complicates the policing of Macedonia's borders according to United Nations Interim Administration Mission in Kosovo (UNMIK) standards, let alone those of Schengen. Similarly, much remains unknown about the organised criminal gangs running the routes leading to the EU.

It is not known what keeps gang members together, or the relative importance of variables such as ethnicity, race, family, friendship, loyalty or fear. Similarly unknown is the extent to which current generalisations about recruitment and funding are valid across different types of crime or gangs. Lessons are undoubtedly learned, and technologies, tactics and techniques transferred between the various groups, but little is known about how this happens. Much depends on the specific groups concerned and the skills needed to ensure success in their particular lines of business. That the raison d'être for terrorist-sponsored criminals can range from political or religious objectives to simple opportunism probably makes a difference to the required capabilities: migrant trafficking or money laundering may require different capabilities to counterfeiting or property crime. On the other hand, some gangs run a range of businesses, with many of the Albanian gangs operating across the Adriatic, combining trafficking in women, weapons, tobacco and heroin. Albanians also act as intermediaries for the Colombian criminals smuggling cocaine, or as export agents for cannabis from Italy to the Netherlands and other EU countries. And they do so very successfully: EUROPOL's 2003 report on organised crime lists ethnic-Albanian criminals as 'among the main threats to the EU' and ahead of organised-crime groups from other parts of the former Yugoslavia.[19]

Some criminal groups operate using seemingly legitimate businesses and some operate in the shadows, offering consultancy services to other groups that lack the expertise or border-related connections necessary for successful operations within the EU. Even so, the more successful of the various groups probably have much in common. Core capabilities are likely to include the exploitation of illegal networks, dedication to the pursuit of profit (this is a prime motivator for most criminals), and the willingness to corrupt and use violence and intimidation. Thus the pursuit of profit permits Albanian traffickers in people, heroin and cigarettes to work with Serbs, Montenegrins, Russians and Italians regardless of ethnic considerations. An easy resort to violence is also evident, as in 2001 when gangs smuggling cigarettes through the border region between Kosovo, Macedonia and Serbia fought Macedonian police for several days after the police tried to break up their networks.

However, more would be needed for organised crime to benefit from and fund such activities – and avoid prosecution. Profits must be concealed, disguised or somewhat legitimised. Not only are the most successful criminals likely to have political connections but they are also likely to be ruthless and intellectually agile, as well as profit-driven and opportunistic. Their ability to diversify in the face of new business opportunities implies adaptive capabilities, whether intellectual or operational. New ways will be used to commit old crimes and new methods will be developed to exploit new opportunities. This has serious implications for the EU. In other words, the main methods used by the smugglers of narcotics, people, or goods into the EU may be known, but the nature and scale of the problem are not fully understood, let alone quantifiable.

Ultimately, what matters most is that the Balkans represent a hub for transnational organised crime. Their geographical position means that they are a politically fragile transit zone for the illegal trafficking of people and goods to the EU. Effective or improved border security hinders trafficking, but this is a rare capability in Balkan countries. In other words, the Balkans will continue to play an important role in the EU's security calculations for the foreseeable future: 'organised crime and corruption is a real obstacle to democratic stability, the rule of law, economic development and development of civil society in the region'.[20] Organised crime is in this way an EU and regional, rather than simply national problem, and therefore requires a regional solution. The EU's ability to influence the long-term future of the region fundamentally is however uncertain.

It is therefore more than probable that organised crime in the Balkans will continue to be 'a source of grave concern to the EU'.[21]

This explains the EU's security fears, and its three-fold emphasis on the needs for stability in the region, for improved international intelligence on organised crime, and for cooperation between the various national border forces operating on its periphery. The EU's ultimate objective is to achieve 'European standards' of border management in the region, to 'progressively consolidate the Western Balkans countries' relations with the European Union and to open up a real perspective of adhesion'.[22]

Strategic tools

Improving border management and regional cooperation is a fundamental element in the EU's strategy for achieving these objectives; its formal priorities (and funding) focus on the management of international borders, regional infrastructure development and helping the countries build stronger national institutions. With its desire for stability in the Balkans reinforced by security fears regarding organised crime and terrorism, the EU exerts pressure on the states of the region to improve their record of fighting transnational crime. Alongside this pressure, the EU monitors the progress of the Balkan states and assists them with the implementation processes necessary for effective border security. In this way, it fulfils commitments made at the London conference of 2002 (which promulgated an international strategy for tackling crime in the region) and the Thessaloniki Summit of June 2003. Above all, it means that the EU emphasises the need for regional cooperation; it consistently argues that cooperation is a route to national as well as regional stability and growth, and as such serves the mutual interests of all countries in the region, quite apart from its own member states.

The policy by which close – and coherent – cooperation (that is, 'adhesion' or 'approximation', in EU jargon) between the EU and the region is to be achieved is known as the Stabilisation and Association Process (SAp). SAp, which has been in existence since 1999, refers to the establishment of some form of privileged political and economic relationship between the EU and the countries in the Balkans. SAp does not automatically grant the states concerned the status of applicant countries, but it is an external instrument for integration, offering support for long-term capacity-building. In particular, it promotes a model of 'integrated' border management as a main area of intervention, together with other relevant measures such as institution-building, the development of a regional infrastructure, and twinning arrangements (an agreement between a candidate country and one or more EU member states to transfer Schengen-related skills and knowledge).

States are helped to implement the processes necessary for effective border security through the Community Assistance for Reconstruction, Development and Stabilisation (CARDS) programme. The CARDS programme is the cornerstone of EU policy in the region, as can be seen from the €4,650 million allocated to cover its costs in the 2000–06 period. Ten percent of this sum is used to support broad regional objectives (such as harmonisation with EU norms and approaches or economic development) but the bulk of the funding is channelled towards country programmes – 'Country Strategy Papers'– that address specific national problems. The support focuses on equipment and infrastructure, 'but, as a conditionality, will be complemented by institution building, technical assistance and twinning-type arrangements to ensure coherence, sustainability and the overall enhanced effectiveness of the border control institutions involved'.[23]

The five beneficiary countries are Albania, BiH, Croatia, Serbia and Montenegro (including Kosovo), and Macedonia, each of which require tailored plans. The State Border Service (SBS) in BiH may be consistent with the CARDS approach, but the situations in Kosovo and Albania are very different, not least because both are transit points and sources of illegal migration. In addition, the CARDS programme builds on, rather than replaces, existing initiatives, so its approach in BiH, for example, is to provide additional resources for existing cooperation arrangements with Croatia on topics such as priority crossings. Most of the CARDS to Albania and BiH is managed by the EC's in-country delegations, though assistance to Macedonia is managed by the European Agency for Reconstruction (EAR). The CARDS programme does not operate in Slovenia.

In other words, the CARDS programme is implemented nationally but aims to ensure that its national strategies support regional coherence. It does this by promoting and funding the development of common approaches and technical specifications. It also emphasises the EC's commitment to 'the inviolability of borders, territorial integrity and sovereignty of the countries of the region'.[24] This suggests that the EU's interest in burden-shifting is of less immediate functional consequence than its conviction that effective security requires a degree of mutual trust based on a shared understanding of what is necessary.

This conviction also underpins the consistent emphasis of CARDS programmes on the need for coordination at national and international levels. It is reflected in the prevalence of statements suggesting that national coordination 'between border control authorities, national police authorities and customs agencies is highly productive in strengthening border controls, including sharing of information and joint investigations'.[25] It is also evident in the stress placed on preventive (information exchange) and reactive (joint investigation) components of international coordination. In practice, most countries accept CARDS programmes because they seek good relations with the EU, rather than with their neighbours. While their functional standards fall far short of EU ideals, most states are consequently in the process of developing or implementing strategies for border management. Even so, most senior officers –directors of border services, deputy directors, chiefs of service, chiefs of staff, and their equivalent – promote cooperation (rather than a more formal coordination) between neighbouring border guards, as well as joint-training courses and facilities. More importantly, their anticipatory planning is invariably based on the so-called Schengen principles.

Guidelines for the EU's preferred model of border management were laid down in the Schengen acquis, which establishes the written rules and commonly accepted standards for border management within the Schengen sphere. The acquis was integrated into the EU framework in 1999 (when the Treaty of Amsterdam came into force).[26] Schengen addresses the legal basis for action, as well as the definition and demarcation of borders, border-crossing procedures, the aim and content of border checks, details of acceptable travel documents, and visa policies and practices. It emphasises the need for a clear division of tasks between authorities, placing the control of people crossing external borders, for instance, with authorised officials, and establishing the illegality of external border-crossings at any point other than an official border post. Cooperation between guards is regarded as essential.

According to Schengen, border security is a matter of law enforcement, not national defence. It is to be delivered by a professional, specialist, multipurpose border police with a dedicated and unified command chain, rather than by military troops or conscripts. Following Schengen standards, this police force is to be answerable to a ministry of the interior rather than defence, the policing methods used must be understandable to those crossing borders, and the officers concerned must be accountable to legislatures, specialised parliamentary committees and other executive authorities.

The acquis is supplemented by the Schengen Catalogue, which provides guidance on what is politically acceptable to the EU. This comprises 'recommendations' and 'best practices' rather than legally binding documents, and sets out the EU's understanding of the optimal way for countries to reach its standards. The introduction states that it will 'serve as a reference tool for future evaluations undertaken in the candidate countries', though in practice it is more influential than this suggests.[27]

Schengen represents the gold standard in border control. Achieving anything like its standards demands a significant administrative capacity, which is often lacking in South-east Europe. It requires a coherent national strategy and the creation of a specialised and trained guard force with adequate financing and resources and effective command-and-communications structures. Schengen standards emphasise that the functions and tasks of border security must not be fragmented amongst authorities, that guards should not be the target of political disputes, or politicians' personal ambitions, and that political controversies (concerning, for example, the location of a border) should not be allowed to disrupt normal border control.

Though this ideal is rarely implemented in the Balkans, the stated aims and objectives of the EU are widely known. The obligations associated with Schengen's standards may apply only to member states, but in practice they form the basis of a European standard of border management to which countries in South-east Europe formally aspire. It is true that only BiH and Slovenia have systems that closely reflect or are compatible with EU standards, and that most Balkan countries (Albania and Macedonia in the case of this paper) are only now considering the strategies and measures required to develop one. Even so, most senior guards accept that it is desirable to use (or at least acknowledge) EU standards as the basic criteria for the future development of their states' border controls.

In practice, EC proposals to assemble a common corpus of relevant legislation are followed by most if not all senior border guards in the region, with the result that European standards of border management are now emerging.[28] Even Albania and Macedonia know that EU proposals will introduce certain mandatory 'good practices' in the existing Common Manual for External Borders, and that these will exert political pressure on their border standards. They cannot ignore EU specifications for legal frameworks and procedures. Nor can they dismiss as politically irrelevant the EU's introduction of complex common mechanisms for operational consultation and cooperation, and techniques for integrated risk evaluation.

Schengen standards are complex and demanding, and there are naturally differences of understanding and acceptance across the region, especially regarding operational notions such as providing service to citizens. This is most noticeable in relation to the guidance and assistance elements of the EU's ideal model. Guards within the EU's direct sphere of influence are trained in the rights and protection of asylum-seekers, in commonality and are also directed to respect the dignity and human rights of illegal migrants or petty smugglers, none of which makes much sense to the typical guard at a checkpoint on Macedonia's borders with Albania or Serbia. Resources and capacity differ too, as well as organisation. BiH has specialist mobile units capable of supporting regular units whereas Macedonia does not, as such units require a high degree of operational flexibility and logistical support.

Nevertheless, regional progress has been made towards a common understanding of EU requirements; problems have been acknowledged, as has the need to develop appropriate cooperative measures. Even Albania, with its notoriously low levels of border security, is developing links with its neighbours, as shown in the opening of a number of border crossings in late 2003. Albania is keen, for example, to show that it actively patrols its border with Macedonia, that it is developing appropriate services, and that it is strengthening its national investigative capacity to tackle crime and illegal migration on its borders. In the meantime, Macedonia has welcomed a new EU police mission, Proxima, which was initiated by the EU's special representative in Macedonia in early 2004 with the aim of helping Macedonia fight organised crime along its borders with Albania, Kosovo and Serbia. Proxima also forms part of EU measures intended to reform the Macedonian Ministry of the Interior (MoI) and create a border police force, as much of Macedonia's border security is currently an army responsibility.

The EU's influence in Albania and Macedonia, as elsewhere in the Balkans, is a product of its unparalleled assistance to the region, which ensures that senior guards in the countries concerned take CARDS programmes, the acquis and the Catalogue very seriously. This trend is further reinforced by a series of JHA projects (funded by the various CARDS's national programmes) that provide guidance, improve the effectiveness of border guards and customs officials, and strengthen regional-cooperation structures so as to raise the status of border guards relative to other security forces. Apart from the CARDS programmes, the means of turning goodwill and tolerance into compatibility with Schengen's standards include IBM programmes and assistance from organisations such as the International Centre for Migration Policy Development (ICMPD), the OSCE and the Stability Pact.

Integrated Border Management

The CARDS programme promotes the IBM management model, which is seen as a method of increasing the trust and cooperation necessary for transferring Schengen-style border security to South-east Europe, and as a means by which the EU can deepen its defences. Its political importance is evident from the €17m allocated to its development in the CARDS regional budget for the 2001–04 period.

The IBM programme is promoted by the CARDS system because of its holistic approach to border management. Guards need to cooperate when managing shared national borders, while border crossings cannot control people or crime unless the guards concerned also cooperate with other agencies, including customs, central ministries and veterinary agencies. In other words, the IBM programme explicitly addresses the fact that border-management problems cannot be solved at the border alone. It is also used by governments and senior officers (formally and informally) to show that they are actively developing standards consistent with the EU's objectives; used in this sense, IBM either symbolises the aspirations of organisations or legitimises reform measures.

IBM is an ambiguous topic. As far as the CARDS programme is concerned, it is an approach rather than a specific model. As such, it 'tackles in a comprehensive way the interrelated problems of trade and traffic bottlenecks at border crossings, insecurity, crime and smuggling across borders and, where relevant, the development problems of the border regions themselves'.[29] And an IBM programme 'requires the numerous authorities and agencies involved in these areas (especially border control and customs) to work together on common problems, rather than working separately and often at cross purposes'.[30] Some form of 'integrated' or coherent and comprehensive border management is thought essential when, for example, neighbouring countries must prioritise their main border, agree on common approaches to border security, or develop cooperation programmes in regions that cross borders. The inclusion of an IBM programme is judged essential in cross-border regional-infrastructure strategies that require agreement between countries in the region, EU member states and candidate countries.

On the other hand, IBM also requires specific forms of bureaucratic support because it is not, as far as the EU is concerned, the same as a regionally supported CARDS-type programme. The IBM programme

> ...*requires a different approach. Border management problems are regional... and so must be programmed in a regionally coherent manner and then coordinated during implementation at the international level. To this end, a small allocation for coordination has been made and will be managed centrally.*[31]

The Schengen *Catalogue* presents a slightly different perspective. According to the latter, the IBM model refers to:

> ...*the system covering all aspects of border policy. This system is spread over four complementary tiers (filters) which are: activities in third countries, countries of origin and transit, bilateral and international cooperation, measures at the external borders and further activities inside the territory.*[32]

The Catalogue offers a five-step guide to the attainment of Schengen standards. Step 0 involves the development of a series of benchmarks for evaluating future performance. Step 1 requires a presentation of the situation in relation to the benchmarks of Step 0. Step 2 consists of a plan based on a specific timetable. It involves a list of objectives, institutions and times for meeting the EU's legislative and regulatory requirements, the conclusion of memoranda of understanding, and the development of implementation capabilities (such as the addition of new guard towers or detention centres to existing infrastructure). Step 3 refers to the functional division-of-action plans, and a detailed estimate of the personnel and financial resources needed to achieve the objectives. Step 4 is an evaluation of the implemented action plan, the monitoring of its results, and the identification of further requirements. Completion of the documentation tells the EU that appropriate capacity for Schengen-style border management exists and can be further developed.

The term 'IBM' is also used descriptively (especially in the Balkans) to refer to international and national cooperation, coordination, and the integration of the various processes, procedures and actors involved in delivering Schengen-style border security. In addition, it describes occasions when a variety of security-related resources are brought together for the purposes of border security at major border crossings, or to the border management that results from cooperation among key national agencies (border guards or police, customs, and phytosanitary and veterinary controls) and their counterparts in neighbouring countries. Used in this sense, it is an umbrella term that incorporates a number of desirable characteristics. It is also sometimes applied to agreements between neighbouring countries on issues of common concern. Its value in this context is in boosting levels of cooperation and coordination, both of which are necessary for effective and coherent border management. It is also an attractive concept, as neither 'cooperation' nor 'coordination' are precisely defined (thereby allowing variable interpretations of the terms), though cooperation tends to be seen as involving working parties, while coordination is usually described as involving sharing information and joint investigations.

Cooperation is seen as particularly important by the EU, both in terms of interagency cooperation between border control and, for example, customs, and with regard to relations between SAp countries and their EU and candidate-country neighbours.[33] Formal cooperation usually begins with the creation of an interagency working group that includes guards, police and customs, and the development of a strategy and work plan. Three types of interagency cooperation are thought to be especially useful: coordinated processing at border crossings (together with a clear understanding as to who checks what and in what sequence); integrated information-technology systems that include intelligence from guards, national police, and customs; and the acceptance of joint responsibilities. Agreements between countries as to which common borders and crossings take priority and regarding the coordination of controls are encouraged.

Coordination between border authorities, national police and customs agencies is understood as a means of strengthening border controls, while international coordination is defined as working at the preventive level (such as the exchange of information) and at the reactive level (joint investigations against smuggling, for example).

Both cooperation and coordination are invariably presented by the EU as means to greater efficiency and effectiveness. Integrating the various elements involved may not, of course, automatically increase efficiency, but it is thought by most EU officials and senior guards to enable countries to deal with related problems in a comprehensive and coherent (that is, more effective) manner. It is anticipated that such integration will link effective border-security systems, national-police structures and migration-management authorities, and facilitate the physical demarcation of agreed national borders. The key to achieving this is thought by the EU to lie in strategic planning and cooperation, even if in practice resources and infrastructure tend to be as, if not more, important. Nonetheless, the importance of institution-building is emphasised, as are the technical assistance and twinning arrangements necessary for coherence, sustainability and effectiveness.

'IBM' is, in this way, used as both prescription and description. To the EU, its descriptive role is particularly useful in South-east Europe because it keeps channels open with countries that are unlikely to harmonise their border security with Schengen standards for the foreseeable future. Used in this dual sense, the broad approach of the IBM programme accommodates the peculiarities of, for example, the external borders between the five SAp countries (i.e. the land and maritime borders between Albania, BiH, Croatia, Macedonia, Serbia and Montenegro), and between EU states and candidate countries. However, it also offers more focused guidance based on a three-pronged strategy that emphasises the importance of controlling major border-crossing points, developing institutional and technical aspects of state-border systems, and strengthening the capacity of border guards to address crime and uncontrolled migration.

International assistance

International technical assistance plays an important role in improving the capacity needed to achieve such goals. A network of international consultants (often comprising recently retired senior guards) working on behalf of international organisations such as the ICMPD delivers much advice, as do commercial consultancies such as the Netherlands-based TC Team Consult, which specialises in change management. ICMPD, for example, is an intergovernmental organisation based in Vienna intended to promote comprehensive and sustainable migration policies and to serve as an information-exchange mechanism for governments and organisations. ICMPD also acts on behalf of the EC and the Stability Pact for South Eastern Europe, both of which emphasise the need for sustained multilateral efforts in managing migration and, by extension, effective border management in the five SAp countries. Moreover, ICMPD provides the secretariat of the International Task Force for the Cooperation and Development of Border Management in South East Europe. This was created in May 2001 following a meeting organised by the Budapest Process addressing illegal migration. The Budapest Process itself is a consultative forum of approximately 40 governments and ten international organisations and aims to prevent 'irregular' migration in the wider European region. Its informal and flexible nature makes it a useful tool for promoting the EU's approach to immigration control.

In addition, ICMPD offers border-related training and technical assistance. Starting in 2000, for example, it ran a series of training seminars for managers in Macedonia, the aim of which was to introduce relevant officers to the EU acquis concerning migration, asylum, visa and border control. A third and final seminar in Sarajevo in 2001 invited representatives from the region's guarding systems to discuss cooperation in the management of illegal migration, and the upgrading and alignment of their respective border systems to EU standards.

ICMPD has an impressive record of providing high-quality technical expertise. It has conducted, or is conducting, assessments of the financial, organisational and administrative records and capacities of border services in Albania, Macedonia and, most recently, BiH.[34] In the case of BiH, it acted in partnership with TC Team Consult on behalf of the EC and the government of BiH. Its review, launched in December 2003, of the financial sustainability and functional efficiency of the SBS and BiH police force was intended to strengthen the rule of law in BiH and contribute significantly to the reform of its public administration. The consortium reached its conclusions after having used a SWOT analysis to identify the strengths, weaknesses, opportunities and threats of BiH's current system. The SWOT analysis was validated in a workshop attended by representatives from the SBS and BiH police forces in the spring of 2004, and the final report was submitted in May 2004.

ICMPD's work complements that of other intergovernmental organisations such as the OSCE and Stability Pact, which also wish to influence regional border security. The OSCE's contribution focuses on areas such as the civilian aspects of training, assistance for institution-building (especially when national and regional coordinating bodies are involved), and the promotion of cross-border bilateral cooperation. This focus could expand, given the OSCE's self-proclaimed status as 'the largest regional security organisation in the world basing its activities mainly on its comprehensive and co-operative approach to security'.[35] Additionally, the deputy US representative to the OSCE has argued that the organisation should play a more positive role in Balkan border security, one that goes beyond its existing work in travel-document security, the Balkan Border Conference, and border-guard training-and-monitoring operations. In other words, the US is now encouraging the OSCE to work more closely with international organisations to 'explore the development of a coordinated action plan to help [OSCE] states enhance their own border management and security efforts'.[36]

The Stability Pact, meanwhile, supports initiatives in civilian-military cooperation and groups working on border and visa issues under MARRI (Migration, Asylum, Regional Return Initiative), whose self-declared objective is 'to enhance state and human security and initiate, facilitate and coordinate developments in the fields of asylum, migration, visa, border management and sustainability of return and to meet international and European standards'.[37] Its intention is to assist countries to fulfil their relevant SAp obligations and to foster bilateral and regional cooperation in general. It works closely with SAp and CARDS projects.

The approaches adopted by the EU, ICMPD, OSCE and Stability Pact have much in common. All see the successful implementation of practical short-term measures as the basis for the international community's medium-term political goals and objectives for the region. Consequently, plans for Macedonia promote police-based border management but also acknowledge the need to train and certify the military personnel currently involved in border-control and anti-trafficking activities. More generally, countries in the region are expected to state their national policies and strategies for IBM, define their national action plans, and establish national coordinating structures and procedures. Examples of the latter include internal, bilateral and multilateral mechanisms and procedures for exchanging information on border and trafficking issues. Such objectives are possible because of the functional and regional consensus that exists regarding appropriate styles of guarding.

Common assumptions and principles

When allied to the special environment and culture in which border tasks are to be performed, the roles played by the EU, CARDS, and ICMPD ensure that Europe's border guards share a common vocabulary. Border security is widely understood as comprising tasks and missions such as the provision of security filters and cross-border cooperation. It is increasingly defined as a specialised form of police work, performed at the national external borders (land, sea and airports), and covering tasks such as entry-and-exit control, the prevention of illegal entry, the combating of alien smuggling and the narcotics trade, and police functions in border regions.

At the senior level at least, consensus also results from the publicly stated conviction that uncontrolled migration and transnational organised crime threaten South-east Europe as a whole. Other areas of consensus concern the need for bilateral agreements. Procedures are often unsatisfactory (few countries keep records of aliens applying for a visa or residence permit, for example) but bilateral agreements are generally seen as an important way of dealing with removal, repatriation and readmission; the United Nations High Commissioner for Refugees (UNHCR) regulates asylum claims in BiH while Macedonia has bilateral agreements with a number of states. The countries of South-east Europe also acknowledge Schengen's insistence on information exchange and national and local liaison officers. Indeed, a survey conducted by the Geneva Centre for the Democratic Control of Armed Forces (DCAF) in 2003 suggests that most countries regard cooperation as critical for the development of effective national and regional border security. Further, the means by which this is to be achieved are invariably thought to include joint border-surveillance systems, joint-assessment systems, joint-training centres, networks of liaison officers, and a common terminology. This represents a shared regional understanding that is explicitly shaped by Schengen principles and objectives.

A degree of unanimity now exists regarding the organisational and functional variables needed for 'professional', 'European' border management – the terms are used synonymously amongst senior officers and both confer status on guarding – yet significant differences remain. Border services differ according to variables such as legacy issues (the inheritance of war or specific traditions), geopolitical circumstances, organisational choices whereby forces are centralised or regionalised, social conditions, and functional imperatives. Of the various factors, EU initiatives are probably the most positive influence, and social realities the most negative. Even so, the balance between the variables is nuanced, because tensions exist at a number of levels. There is often, for example, a gap between international and regional assumptions. The stresses resulting from the role of NATO are particularly significant. NATO plays a subordinate role in regional border security but continued insecurity (and NATO's links to the US) means that its role remains significant. Thus, both control and protection underlie the international consensus on the need for reform.

Control and protection

The need for control is self-evident, but that for protection is more controversial. Control is acceptable because the Balkans are a gateway to the EU for illegal trafficking, the management of which is seen by the EU (and by many guards in the Balkans) as an enforcement or policing matter. However, certain internationally desirable borders (such as that between Macedonia and Serbia) remain contested and require protection by military or paramilitary forces. The result is, as Jonas Widgren, the then director of the ICMPD, noted in 2002, that two parallel lines of action exist at the multilateral level.[38] Whereas the EU emphasises control, NATO favours protection. The EU speaks of the need for 'sound border control and management in the context of the SA process [SAp] and in the perspective of the further integration of the five countries in the EU JHA... structures'.[39] To this end, it uses the CARDS resources described above. In addition, SAp countries know what control involves because they have access to the 2002 Catalogue of recommendations for the correct application of the Schengen acquis and best practices, which was originally intended for candidate countries. In contrast, NATO is primarily concerned with short-term military-based protection and surveillance. Even so, its influence should not be underestimated, for joining its outreach programme (Partnership for Peace) is considered a stepping-stone to alliance membership.

NATO

The EU and NATO are technically partners within South-east Europe, but their roles are not equal; not only are the EU and NATO looking at different types of risk but these risks are also not spread equally across the geographical region. Context is important, as is politics. Thus the security situation in BiH is now judged sufficiently stable to allow NATO's Stabilisation Force in Bosnia and Herzegovina (SFOR) mission to be replaced by a new EU security mission, codenamed Athena, at the end of 2004. Many of Athena's forces will, however, still come from NATO, and NATO will play a key role under the asset-sharing arrangements known as 'Berlin plus', whereby EU-led crisis-management operations have access to NATO assets and planning capabilities.[40] Comparable arrangements apply in Macedonia.

More to the point, such arrangements acknowledge that while EU-style border policing is appropriate on many of BiH's and Macedonia's border crossings, it cannot manage the gangs, 30- or 40-strong and armed with missile launchers and Kalashnikovs, operating in the triangle formed by Albania, Serbia, Kosovo and

Macedonia. Nor can it manage the levels of violence seen in Kosovo in March 2004 during riots by Albanian youths, extremists and criminals, which left at least 31 people dead. Indeed, in the aftermath of these riots, some international commentators argued that the presence of NATO's Kosovo Force (KFOR) at Kosovo's border crossings should be reinforced, along with the province's border security in general.[41] In the event, NATO deployed an extra 1,000 troops to Kosovo, bringing its forces there to about 20,000. The conflict centred on the town of Mitrovica, but was evident in other areas, and in the days following the riots, KFOR mounted joint patrols with the Kosovo Police Service and Kosovo Protection Corps along Kosovo's border with Macedonia. NATO's presence on this land border remains politically and functionally necessary.

Given the security vacuum evident in such areas, NATO's role can be seen as representing a temporary complementarity[42] before full EU standards of civilian authority and tight coordination can be applied. This is not problematic per se, and EU officials usually argue that IBM can accommodate a military role in such circumstances. Not only is it accepted that EU ideals may need to be temporarily adjusted in politically sensitive areas, but some officials also claim that this will offer a firm basis for further cooperation in border security.[43] Indeed, the position of the EU and EC is that such an arrangement is a both realistic and acceptable means for achieving security. On the other hand, the reintroduction of a military presence is seen within the region as a retrograde and destabilising move: the EU advocates border security as a civilian task yet promotes the role of the military when it suits its interests.

Military methods of guarding differ from those promoted by the EU. Troops are not usually trained or equipped to perform police tasks, yet NATO remains involved in many border-related aspects of regional development. Thus UNMIK chose to justify its inclusion in border-security talks in 2003 on the basis that it provides an interim administration for Kosovo. Further, it was the North Atlantic Council that promoted the conference on border management and security in Ohrid in May 2003 that was hosted by Macedonia and supported by the EU, Stability Pact, and OSCE. Indeed, Ohrid's focus on border management (and anti-trafficking operations in Albania, Macedonia, and Serbia and Montenegro/Kosovo) rather than demarcation issues is indicative of NATO's priorities. So too was NATO's willingness to reach agreement with its three international partner institutions (the EU, Stability Pact, and OSCE) on the common political goals, objectives, principles and procedures to which the states concerned could then subscribe. However, Ohrid also reaffirmed the need for a regional approach to border security, and local and regional ownership.

The Ohrid conference suggests that the role of international military forces within border security –is under certain circumstances regarded as legitimate; the use of regional military forces is, however, actively discouraged. This understanding is reinforced by NATO's role in a joint EU and OSCE working group (under the umbrella of the Stability Pact, though initiated by NATO), which aims to develop a coherent approach to border security and management, especially when military units are involved. Even so, it is difficult not to conclude that while NATO and the EU are often mutually supportive, they have different aims and objectives. Moreover, while officials from the two organisations may be in agreement, those from the region often take a harsher view of what is seen as evidence of double standards on the part of the EU, which tolerates NATO's involvement but insists that involving indigenous military forces in guarding is unacceptable.

In practice, trends, options, and issues of convergence and divergence are best seen in terms of specific regional examples. Research on guarding is limited by the political sensitivity of the topic and the evasive nature of the organisations concerned, but representative examples help to explain how the various actors and agencies involved understand the predicaments resulting from international pressure. Examples suggest how and why those involved invent specific strategies that allow them to accommodate, subvert or evade threats. In particular, they illustrate the strategies, principles, options, and problems typically confronting new or transitional services, as well as the problems associated with devising appropriately democratic standards of border control.

Chapter 2

Bosnia Herzegovina and Slovenia

One result of the break-up of Tito's Yugoslavia was the creation of five distinct state-border systems. Three are presented here as exemplifying major trends in regional guarding: BiH's State Border Service (SBS, or Drzavna Granigna Sluba, DGS) reflects the country's status as an internationally managed composite state, Slovenia's approach is unique but also arguably the most successful in the region, while border security in ethnically divided Macedonia is fragile and fragmented. This chapter focuses on the state-border systems of BiH and Slovenia; Chapter 3 tackles that of Macedonia and compares the first three systems to that of Albania, where border security has little meaning.

The strategic and adaptive processes involved in creating effective, efficient and internationally acceptable forms of border security are particularly evident in BiH and Slovenia. Both countries are small and have challenging land borders. In BiH, the Dinaric Alps run from the north-west to the south-east; two-thirds of the country is mountainous with the only flat open country in the north. Slovenia's geography is more varied but equally challenging, with mountains, valleys and rivers to the east, a small coastal strip on the Adriatic, and an alpine region alongside Italy and Austria.

The two countries have numerous problems in common. Both are transit routes for illegal migration and trafficking, and both are vulnerable to legacy issues such as political corruption and a lack of transparency. Major towns may have expensive cars, hotels and retail outlets but away from the main urban centres, subsistence agriculture ensures that many (especially in BiH) live in conditions of considerable hardship. Even so, the difference between the two countries is marked. BiH may have the most sophisticated system of border management in South-east Europe, but it is dependent on international support and its thriving informal economy is accompanied by significant problems of social exclusion. Slovenia has high levels of inflation and an inflexible labour market, but unemployment is low, its budget deficit has been cut, the agricultural sector modernised, and its border police are amongst the most effective in South-east Europe.

The relationship between these factors has yet to be assessed, but the effectiveness of the two countries' border management is probably linked to their economic and political standing. This is evident in their EU status. The goal of BiH is full integration into the EU through the SAp, the main instrument of which is a Stabilisation and Association Agreement (SAA) under which applicants can introduce, adopt, and implement the Schengen acquis and other transitional regulations.[1] The SAA uses border management to facilitate the trade and regional cooperation necessary for the EU's integration project. However, de-industrialised BiH, where nearly half the workforce is unemployed and international aid is being reduced, has little hope of becoming an applicant country. In contrast, prosperous Slovenia, with a per capita income some 70% of the EU average, joined the Union (and thus became part of the EU's external border) in May 2004.

Despite such differences, both BiH and Slovenia are, for various reasons, widely regarded as success stories. BiH's border service represents the region's first state-level, multi-ethnic law-enforcement agency, while Slovenia's border controls are fully harmonised with EU standards. The border systems concerned are otherwise quite distinct, illustrating two strategic options available for effective, efficient and politically acceptable forms of border management within the EU's sphere of influence. BiH is used here to show the role of border management as an aspect of state formation, while Slovenia illustrates the importance of political will in capacity-building.

State Border Service of BiH

The SBS of BiH is important for three reasons: it is new, it is explicitly shaped by political imperatives, and its formal objectives and organisation are based on internationally acceptable norms, structures, and objectives.

BiH's land boundaries are 1,459km in length, of which 932km are shared with Croatia, 527km with Serbia and Montenegro, and 20km are coastline. There are 432 formal locations where it is possible to cross BiH's borders (legally or otherwise), including road entry points, airports and railway crossings. Before the civil war of 1992–95, Serbs made up 40% of the population, Muslims 38% and Croats 22%, but the current ethnic composition is unknown.

International interests

The initial impetus behind the creation of the SBS is difficult to identify, but it seemingly owes much to the determination of the then Special Representative of the United Nations Secretary-General, the American Jacques Klein.[2] Klein was convinced that BiH, as a new country, required a service that could control its porous borders and thereby preserve its sovereignty, territorial integrity, political independence and 'international personality'.

Klein's aggressive approach to state-building reflected that of the international community. The requirement for a BiH state-border police was first raised at the December 1997 Peace Implementation Council in Bonn, and the drafting of preliminary legislation by the Office of the High Representative (OHR – the chief civilian peace implementation agency), the UN's International Police Task Force (IPTF) and BiH authorities took place in the months that followed. After the repeated failure of BiH's State Parliament to promulgate the Law on the State Border Service, in January 2000 the High Representative (at that time Carlos Westendorp) finally imposed a border-service directorate designed to enforce BiH law on the SBS. The State Parliament ratified the law in the summer of 2001, a number of SBS units were inaugurated in the following months and a dedicated training centre opened in May 2001. By 2002, staff levels were at approximately 1,400, divided between a headquarters and 15 units. There are now 2,400 border police; 10% perform administrative duties, and each sector has an inner reserve of 10%. About 98% of state-border crossings are covered.

International commitment to the success of the SBS is reflected in the Service's title, budget and the work conditions of its guards. By early 2003, the total deployment budget was US$28.3m, of which 61% was allocated for salaries, 15% for allowances, 11% for operating costs, and 13% for capital budget. Salaries range from €648 per month for the director and his deputies, to approximately €240 for the most complex jobs performed by officers with low educational standards.

The political and financial resources invested in the SBS are evident. The UN Mission in Bosnia Herzegovina (UNMIBH)'s Border Service Department (BSD), for instance, controlled the Service's early development and management. This helped control the drafting and implementation of border legislation and the development of the SBS' legal foundation. It also ensured that the SBS' integrated border-control management model was based on EU standards, and that its equipment and training reflected international standards and approaches. The SBS's reliance on international aid is understandable in the circumstances, for the SBS inherited little in the way of resources or extensive equipment, and training programmes were badly needed: pre-war BiH lacked an international border or border force, so the new guards had no experience of controlling international borders, identifying forged documents, or dealing with illegal immigration.[3] Many countries, including Austria, Germany, Hungary, Italy, the Netherlands, Sweden, Switzerland, the UK and the USA, quickly provided bilateral financial assistance, donations, and training programmes.

The SBS' formal organisation and objectives reflect the philosophy of such donors, for whom democratic forms of border management in BiH are a normative priority, a legitimising principle and an organising device. Assistance is seen as a means of ensuring that BiH has the working structures and capacity needed to function as a state, meet the challenges of combating transnational organised crime, grasp the opportunities offered by the SAp, deter illegal migrants, and act as an external line of defence for the EU. These objectives are given practical expression in training packages, such as standard UNMIBH courses that include advice on 'human dignity'. The UNHCR, meanwhile, provides training in the handling of asylum seekers, while the EU's UK-led IMMPACT team trained more than 1,500 officers in forgery detection, interviewing and profiling during the SBS' first two years.[4] International objectives are also reflected in recent EU announcements that its police-training mission in BiH will train the police in border control, and that customs regulations are to be harmonised with the EU by 2005.

Lastly, the creation of the SBS resulted from the international community's determination to create a showcase for an autonomous multi-ethnic police force. The EU has emphasised BiH's overall need to strengthen its capacity in the fields of justice and home affairs, and the SBS is seen as an important contribution towards police reform. The SBS is accordingly described as a specialist police force and categorised as a law-enforcement agency. Its duties include discovering and preventing indictable offences, searching for those committing them, investigating border-related criminal offences within its jurisdiction, supervising the state border, ensuring security at BiH's airports, and controlling official crossing points. Through the European Union Police Mission (EUPM) – which succeeded the UN's IPTF as the EU's chosen means for establishing sustainable border policing – the EU has sought to establish a sustainable model of policing (including border policing) that is in accordance with EU standards and European practice more generally. This is achieved through various monitoring, mentoring and inspection activities, such as those associated with the CARDS programme, which supports the EUPM's work and provides aid to the SBS. In other words, the SBS fulfils multiple objectives.

Strategic options

The SBS strategy is designed with four major objectives in mind:

- To achieve Schengen-type border control in terms of security and increased awareness
- To achieve harmonisation with EU border-control and customs regulations by 2005
- To curtail illegal migration to Western Europe
- To control BiH's borders while contributing significantly to the effective collection of customs-and-excise revenue by chan-nelling goods to customs points, diverting traders to legitimate crossings where duties can be levied.

The two fundamental themes shaping the development of the SBS are security and state-building. The first theme, security, is critical. BiH is a springboard to the EU for illegal migrants and organised crime, and the SBS is intended to act as a filter mechanism for the EU's own security. The functions of the SBS were accordingly defined as including the supervision of state-border and airport security, control over state-border crossings, the detection and prevention of indictable offences and apprehending those committing them, and investigating border-related criminal offences within the border jurisdiction (10km); the offences concerned are mainly those of organised crime, smuggling, illegal migration, trafficking and corruption. It was thought essential that the new service should possess operational flexibility, mobility, strong investigative and intelligence capabilities, and a proficient IT network and data server. Ambassador Klein consistently stressed the need for international cooperation, which meant that importance was always attached to the exchange of information, readmission agreements, joint-control zones, joint patrols, and joint intelligence and investigation between BiH and its neighbours.

Second, the SBS represents an experiment in both state- and institution-building. International assistance to BiH's institutions (which was always seen as a matter of fundamental importance) ensured that BiH had the working structures and capacity needed for it to function as a viable country. Added to this assistance was pressure from both the international community and the Entities within Bosnia (the Bosnia-Croat Federation and Republika Srpska) for a 'professional' and multi-ethnic institution. This explains the distinctive management model of the SBS. The Border Services Directorate (BSD) is at the apex of the model, with the Chief of the BSD reporting directly to the commissioner of the IPTF or his equivalent. The SBS Directorate meanwhile consists of three equal directors, one from each ethnic group, who are appointed for a period of four years, with the executive directorship rotating between the three every eight months (the first appointments were made in 2000). This helps avoid the weakness of BiH's state institutions in relation to the entity administrations. The director and his two deputies report to the Council of Ministers on political issues and work closely with the chief of the service. They also supervise the internal control unit of the SBS, which deals with disciplinary problems.

Implementation of the strategy was spread over three phases.[5] The priority in the first phase was to establish and staff the SBS headquarters in Lukavica, to be followed by the inauguration of the SBS at Sarajevo airport, and the handover of three land crossings from the entity police, the Federation cantonal interior ministries, and the Republika Srpska Interior Ministry. Units for established parts of the border zone were formed as distinct spatial internal organisational elements whose jurisdiction covered the tasks of border surveillance, control of state-border crossings, and the detection and prevention of criminal activities directed against either border security or tasks undertaken by the SBS. Developments were in accordance with EU procedures and standards, and were completed on time.

Assumptions and principles

The formal assumptions and principles underpinning the activities of the SBS are common to most European forces. The SBS is a law-enforcement agency adhering to democratic standards in its dealings with the public. It is an independent police, rather than a paramilitary organisation, and its formal working practices derive from its status as an autonomous border-security force, rather than as part of a national police force or the MoI. The SBS acknowledges that recruits need police experience if they are to be effective, so it provides specialised training and a border-security qualification. In this way, it retains some control over its own recruitment, rather than abdicating the responsibility to the MoI.

All military connotations or associations have been sharply rejected, with most senior officers convinced that the presence of military units, let alone military habits, is destabilising and should be dismantled as rapidly as possible. Although NATO attempted to pressurise BiH into using demobilised troops for border police, the IPTF supported the SBS in rejecting the scheme on the basis that border security is a civilian matter. The SBS argued that the two should cooperate where necessary but that responsibility be strictly demarcated, as the military lacks the specific skills that police bring to the job.

Even so, the SBS cannot operate in isolation, and must cooperate with a range of agencies. At the domestic level, these include customs, Ministry of Interior police (MUP), Brcko District police, other agencies for protection and information, legislative bodies, and the EUPM (several of whose projects are relevant to SBS).[6] At the governmental level, SBS is answerable to BiH's council of ministers, rather than a central ministry. At the international level, cooperation is required with BiH's neighbours, particularly Croatia, and with regional work groups, the Southeast European Cooperative Initiative Regional Centre for Combating Transborder Crime (SECI Centre), and with EUROPOL and INTERPOL.

Assessment

Bosnia's politicians are increasingly aware of the importance of border security to both BiH and the EU. Deputy Security Minister Dragan Mektic has repeatedly underlined BiH's determination to adopt European standards regarding terrorism, organised crime, and, by extension, border security.[7] The return to power of nationalist parties in the general elections of July 2002 also implied factional interest in the importance of strong borders.

The SBS is in many respects a success. This is unsurprising, given the political capital and international resources invested in it. The SBS is expensive, but it is amongst the most advanced border systems in the region and its creation is a major achievement. It is highly integrated, and its units have multiple functions. Each has an investigative component, for example, and there are plans to include an intelligence role in the future, though separate units already exist for land-border surveillance. The need for flexibility ensures that two types of small mobile (rapid response) units operate, one covering observation and surveillance, the other information, support and control.

The SBS has enhanced the authority of BiH as a state and increased its revenues; it makes a real contribution to securing financial resources for the budgets of both the State and Entities of BiH. It has been heavily involved in the fight against cross-border crime and uncontrolled migration, thereby acting as a filter mechanism for the EU. In 2000, for example, perhaps as many as 50,000 people passing through Sarajevo airport (thought to be a starting point for thousands of immigrants from Bangladesh, China, Iran, Sri Lanka and Turkey) were unaccounted for, but within 12 months of SBS controls, the figure had dropped to 9,000. On balance, significant progress has been made, especially in relation to illegal migration. With better leadership, training and equipment, many criminal charges are now filed, most of which relate to false documents, smuggling, illegal trade, drugs and so forth.[8]

Nonetheless, problems do exist, some of which are common to the region and some that are unique to BiH. Common issues include:

• *Relations with locals* Effective policing is prejudiced by high unemployment in BiH's rural areas, which encourages smuggling and reduces cooperation.

- *Relations with police* Initiatives appear to be made by the SBS, rather than the police. Indeed, border guards are often barely accepted by the public police and entity-customs officers, who resent their high profile and resources. This has much to do with the fact that guards' salaries are several times higher than those of their counterparts within the police.
- *Resistance to transparency* Residual suspicion remains.
- *Poor management* A state-level body, the Office for Auditing of the Financial Operations of the Institutions of BiH, investigated the SBS and concluded that it must improve its financial management.[9]
- *Migration* Several readmission agreements have been signed, but serious problems remain.

Many internally generated problems are also typical of the region. Vested interests are always problematic, and new security agencies such as the SBS are vulnerable to sabotage, manipulation, or cooption by the agents or structures whose interests are threatened. Not surprisingly, BiH's development is shaped by conflicting political goals that are often supported by corruption. For example, various attempts were made to use entity votes and ethnic control of key areas to sabotage or subvert the SBS during the initial proposals of 1999, while in 2000, the Bosniac nationalist Party of Democratic Action (SDA) argued that electoral losses mattered little provided it retained control of key positions in the border and intelligence services.[10] The ability of international organisations to deal with these issues is limited; the OHR can command, but genuine reform requires support from the domestic authorities. Even so, the monitoring of appointments, financing and training by international officers and officials helped ensure the credibility of the SBS' formal functions and legal framework in its first years.

These problems matter because, as the SBS acknowledges, the Service 'is like a fishing net – it is only as good as the largest hole'.[11] Other problems result from BiH's goal of full integration into the EU. At the end of 2003, the EC said it hoped that BiH would be ready for negotiations on a SAA – the first step towards eventual EU membership – in late 2004. But achieving this will depend on BiH showing major progress in strengthening its central government and reforming its economy and judiciary, all of which impact on border management.[12] Thus, certain land and river/maritime borders have yet to be closed, the mobile-unit concept for documentation and for emergencies needs strengthening, the IT system has yet to be fully connected, and there is an urgent need for training on asylum issues now that BiH is to take over these task from the UNHCR (the asylum unit within the Ministry of Security was supposed to have assumed responsibility for determining refugee status by 30 April 2004, but the deadline was not met). Meeting the EU's terms for launching talks on closer ties will be difficult, and disappointment may affect morale and standards.

Ultimately, however, BiH is atypical because it is the direct result of international responses to regional issues. It remains heavily dependent on massive foreign assistance, though the latter is seldom coordinated. In 2001, for instance, courses teaching specialist-interviewing skills were provided by Denmark, the UK, and the UNHCR working in isolation, while the US Immigration and Naturalisation Service (INS) ignored the UNMIBH's BSD and worked directly with the SBS. This approach remains characteristic.

For the moment, the development of the SBS relies on BiH's role as a European protectorate. The role played by Special Representative Klein in the creation of the SBS was significant, but the level of power wielded by the international community's high representative (who oversees the affairs of state) is extraordinary. Paddy Ashdown has since his appointment as High Representative in May 2002 pursued policies aimed at implementing the economic, legal and governance reforms necessary for both BiH statehood and European integration, all of which impact on the SBS. At the state level, Ashdown has balanced the power of the Bosnian government with that of the entity governments of the Federation (dominated by Muslims and Croats) and Republika Srpska (dominated by Serbs). Power sharing between the groups is mostly symbolic, though it does have meaning in the SBS, whose structure reflects the countries' various decision-making authorities: these comprise the common institutions, and those at the state level, as well as two executive and legislative powers, one for each Entity, plus the special case of the Brcko District. In the circumstances, a unified SBS makes sense.

Even so, the SBS has yet to escape from its social and political environment, and this is more than a simple matter of reform. The SBS has adopted but then failed to implement several strategic documents authored by international groups. The notion that the SBS exists to enforce the law rather than the wishes of the government of the day means little because ideas such as personal accountability are absent from the existing police culture. Corruption, low-quality recruits and incompetence are real problems, as is the powerlessness of the SBS in the face of well-organised smuggling operations enjoying political protection. Similarly, the SBS cannot affect the most profitable forms of organised crime in BiH (human trafficking and smuggling) because they are a regional rather than local problem, and regional cooperation leaves much to be desired. Dealing with the minority communities that dominate border areas is particularly difficult, for their interests are threatened by an effective centralised border service. Similar considerations apply to the ethnic groups' militaries and intelligence agencies (which are to be unified). International pressure for specific forms and standards of border management are, as ever, offset by social and regional realities.

Slovenia

Like BiH, Slovenia sits on an established smuggling route to Western Europe and although arms smuggling had declined by the late 1990s, the country's police force estimates that trafficking in drugs and people increased as the region gained stability. Though Slovenia's criminal networks are closely integrated with those of other ex-Yugoslav countries, there is little else in common. Slovenia is relatively rich and has managed to avoid many of the legacy problems associated with the collapse of Yugoslavia; it had no territorial ambitions to pursue or ethnic divisions to resolve and has long enjoyed close ties with Europe through economic, cultural and migratory links. It is special by virtue of its geographical size and position, its Habsburg heritage, its ethnic coherence (more than 87% of the population is Slovene) and its compliance with EU standards: it became a member state in May 2004.

Background

Slovenia shares 546km of borders with Croatia, 324km with Austria, 235km with Italy, 102km with Hungary and has a coastline of 46km. The country is rural, with extensive areas of forest and grassland. Before the 1991 war of independence, Slovenian police controlled border crossings, while the Yugoslav national army conducted surveillance of the land border. After the war, Slovenia took control of the whole border, and the former border between the two republics became the new state border separating Slovenia from Croatia. This is now the EU's external border.

Slovenia lacks a special border police force. A specialised police unit for border surveillance was established in 2002 (when 100 candidates applied for 30 posts, 16 of which were filled), but border duties are still conducted primarily by specially trained and equipped police units within the regular police.[13]

Strategic options

Slovenia's options were limited by its early decision to seek EU membership, leaving it no choice but to implement the Schengen regime for border management. However, financial pressures, the need for rationalisation, and inexperience meant that the identification of a clear strategy took time. Two distinct phases can be identified.

Preparations for achieving harmonisation with EU standards began early, and a number of significant markers are identifiable during the first phase, which lasted for the first five years of independence. Legislation passed soon after independence in 1991, for example, included a State Border Control Act that not only abolished the old 'border zone' and restrictive movement regime but also established a concept of border control by specialised border-police units, with special control standards being defined for the first time. An initial decision was taken that Slovenia would have one police force, rather than specialised border units. It was the government's belief that the necessary crackdown on illegal migration and smuggling would require close links between conventional police and specialised border units and it therefore appeared counterproductive to develop an independent border-security system. Significantly, the importance of police discretion was established early on, with the objectives of border control expanded to include 'strengthening the subjective responsibility of police officers': that is, the acceptance of personal responsibility.[14] Detailed legislation on foreigners and travel documentation for Slovenian citizens followed.

Considerable effort was devoted to determine Slovenia's needs during the second, screening phase. Consultation, for example, involved examining between ten and 15 different border-security systems and numerous study visits, but this period saw no coherent or coordinated approach to border management; responses were of an ad hoc nature. Even so, it was during this period that Slovenia's distinctive model of border security was developed.

The formal decision to make border policing an integral aspect of the Slovenian police was announced in 1996. The police were divided into three levels (state, region and local), and their functions were based on cooperation between the various units. This proved important because confusion occasionally arose over the division of labour between uniformed and criminal directorates; issue sometimes fell under both border security and crime prevention, or transnational organised crime, or between illegal migration and internal surveillance. The problems were, however, addressed from a border perspective (as opposed to a general policing view), and, in a strategic directional document issued later that year, the Police Directorate emphasised both the collective responsibility for the border and the value of personal responsibility as a critical element of good policing. Police units became responsible for analysing risk levels on their borders.

These developments ushered in a new stage. The government issued a strategic policy document, which stated that Slovenia would implement the Schengen regime. An association agreement was signed in 1996, a national plan for adhering to the acquis was adopted in 1997 and an application for membership made in 1998. The necessary processes of adaptation were reflected in, for example, the Police Act of 1998, which provided the legal framework for a police force as an independent organisation within the MoI. National visa policy was harmonised with that of the EU in 1998. The following year saw the initiation of twinning projects addressing topics such as surveillance (with Germany and Austria), migration (Austria), organised crime (Italy and Spain), and police cooperation (Spain). These projects reinforced the transfer of knowledge to Slovenia, as did visits from JHA experts. The first JHA mission to Slovenia in 1998, for example, identified the priorities (including organised crime) that Slovenia needed to address, while a second, three years later, argued that although the country had made great progress, it still needed to improve the level of its IT equipment so as 'to further professionalize the performance of border control and border surveillance'.[15]

In early 2002, two PHARE Institution Building twinning projects were used to facilitate the necessary harmonisation. The term 'PHARE' reflects the origins of the programme: 'Poland and Hungary Assistance for the Restructuring of the Economy', but it is better understood as a more generalised 'Assistance Programme for Central Europe'. The PHARE programme is one of the three pre-accession instruments financed by the EU to assist applicant countries' preparations for joining the EU, and these projects built on a series of earlier PHARE assistance programmes.[16] Project 22 of the Slovenia National Programme, for example, was designed to reinforce the country's institutional and administrative capacity to adopt and apply the acquis in relation to the control of migration flows at border-inspection posts on the EU's external border. Emphasis was placed on coordination, legal issues, training and on the harmonisation of technical measures, including their type and procurement. The Slovenian police had basic equipment for document control and fraud detection, for example, and an online connection to the MoI's central computer system, but they also needed equipment for detecting concealed people, drugs and weapons. Based on assessments and opinions provided by the project, the Slovenian government defined the developmental and strategic goals and objectives that it needed for a Schengen action plan – to be co-financed by PHARE and achieved by 2005.

Slovenia's determination to harmonise its system with EU standards was evident throughout the screening process in 2000–01. Legislation, for example, was checked for compatibility with the EU, as the EU law system relating to the field of JHA and acquis must be incorporated into national legislation. However, Slovenia chose to undergo the process gradually rather than experience rejection (Poland's action plan had recently been rejected). In the event, Slovenia formally adopted and presented its plan (which included information on visas, infrastructure, data protection, and deployment) in May 2001. By then, it had established a specialised unit for border control that was operational at both state and local levels. An additional specialised unit responsible for border control was created within the General Police Directorate in June 2002.

In this way, technical support from the EU, together with a programme of focused financial support, helped ensure that EU standards for controlling external borders were met. Harmonisation with the acquis was achieved through a new border-surveillance act in 2002, together with the preparation of cadre and equipment plans, new training procedures and compensatory measures and the identification of further necessary legal and technical changes.

Assumptions and principles

As in much of the region, Schengen-style control based on accountability and transparency is a legitimising priority and an organisational device for Slovenia's police. But there are some major differences between Slovenia and its neighbours.

As seen, Slovenia differs from BiH in that it lacks a special independent border police. There are specialised border-police units operating at the local level, but the police units carrying out border tasks are an integral part of the regular police, and border duties are conducted within the framework of public policing. A specialised police unit for border surveillance was created in 2002 but the State Border and Foreigners Section of the Uniformed Police Directorate, which is part of the General Police Directorate, remains responsible for border security. State-border control, surveillance, and the supervision of foreigners are the main tasks of police-border units, but other units, including those used for general police tasks, traffic and more specialised roles (such as dog handlers, mounted units, marine police and airport police) also perform these tasks. In addition, combined police units operate at the local level, providing border checks and surveillance along with all other police tasks within their regional jurisdiction. In all other respects, Slovenia's system is harmonised with Schengen standards.

Slovenia's size and heritage ensure that this distinctive style of border policing works. But one further point also deserves emphasis: the political decision to adopt Schengen standards was an assertion of Slovenia's preferred identity as European, rather than Balkan.

Assessment

Slovenia's system demands a high degree of coordination between all parts of the uniformed police, the criminal police (primarily in relation to organised crime), the operations and communications centre in Ljubljana, and specialised units. That the system works reflects the considerable institutional capacity of Slovenia's police, and the cohesive nature of its society.

The standard of recruits is relatively good, though their small number has caused concern within the EU. In the mid-1990s, the average age of the uniformed police was 31 years, with approximately 7% holding a university degree, 12% with higher education, 67% a high-school education, 8% a professional education, leaving 8% with an elementary education. These statistics provided a good base on which to construct Schengen's action plan for 2001, which required the creation of a new unit within the General Police Directorate specialising in border control. More than 500 new border police were to be recruited. Yet the government's commitment to recruitment has at times appeared hesitant. Only 392 police staff were approved in 2002, and 200 in 2003, instead of the 700 in 2002 and 540 in 2003 called for by the Schengen action plan. The EC's annual report for 2002 revealed that recruitment in 2001–03 fell 600 short of the target of 1,740 new staff. The government's response was to plan for the transfer of customs personnel to the police.

Corruption levels are comparatively low; the Berlin-based Transparency International consistently lists Slovenia as the leading EU membership candidate in terms of combating corruption. Police-community relations are also encouraging, and approximately 10% of calls received by the police relate to border issues. In particular, many suspected illegal migrants are reported to the authorities. When Slovenia faced an influx of more than 35,000 illegal migrants in 2000, good community relations ensured that the police were able to identify, apprehend and return some 42% of those thought to have entered the country. Compared with the same period of the previous year, the number of illegal immigrants apprehended decreased by more than 40% in 2001 and by 68% in the first four months of 2002. By 2002, it was estimated that some 70% of those who had entered in 2001 had been returned.

Nonetheless, illegal migration remains a major problem; Slovenia is both a transit and a destination country. Border-crossing points and police equipment, such as heat-imaging cameras, have been upgraded and police numbers boosted, but international cooperation has also improved since 2000. This is especially noticeable in relation to BiH. Many of the migrants in 2000 (43% of whom were Iranians) had come from BiH or had taken advantage of the relaxation in visa regulations to travel to Slovenia via BiH. Better cross-border cooperation and a stricter visa regime in BiH soon led to a fall in numbers, with arrests dropping to under 21,000 in 2001 and to less than 10,000 in 2002. Slovenia also cooperates closely with Croatia even though the location of the border between the two is disputed and relations have often been acrimonious.

Overall, Slovenia's record is impressive. Significant progress has been made in the areas of data protection, migration, asylum, police cooperation, and organised crime. Dealing with the illegal-drugs trade has proved more problematic, but these difficulties were recognised by the EU during negotiations in the run-up to the Copenhagen summit (where entry conditions for the EU were set), and Slovenia was awarded an extra €107m for border improvements for 2004–06.

Democratic control and personal accountability do not appear to be controversial issues, and morale amongst the police seems reasonably high; it is however difficult to tell the extent to which officers have accepted or merely accommodated reform. Slovenia's EU membership suggests the former but it is entirely possible that the situation has come about because it suits the political interests of ministries or political parties. On the other hand, the cautious nature of the transition suggests thoroughness.

Slovenia's case is special, but its experience provides a useful example of the relative importance in shaping border management of political rationale (EU membership), functional needs (protecting sovereignty and controlling migration), and social-economic conditions (Slovenia being a relatively rich and cohesive society).

Chapter 3

Macedonia and Albania

The security challenges confronting border managers in BiH and Slovenia are essentially those of uncontrolled migration and cross-border crime. They dominate in Albania and Macedonia as well, but are perceived as less problematic by the officers and politicians concerned in these states. The particular political and social conditions in both Albanian and Macedonia, and the gangs of armed insurgents and criminals that ignore the porous borders typical of the two countries, subvert international proposals for effective or democratically accountable styles of border security.

Macedonia

Macedonia was the poorest republic at the time of Yugoslavia's break-up in 1991, when war deprived it of access to important markets and transfer payments. Ten years later, an insurgency resulted in widespread violence, with the result that KFOR now patrols Macedonia's northern border regions, while Macedonian troops remain on alert along the border with Kosovo. Kosovo, meanwhile, is overseen by KFOR and UNMIK, but is in reality ungovernable. Any residual internal stability in the province is threatened by high levels of unemployment (currently at ca. 65%) and endemic criminal activity; indeed, organised crime involving ethnic Albanians underpins its economy. Political tensions, insurgency and illegal trafficking make Macedonia's northern borders dangerous.

Formal border controls are not in the interests of those living on either side of the country's declared borders. The Skopje-Belgrade border agreement of 2001, for example, which redefined the border between Macedonia and Yugoslavia, is a source of bitterness for the ethnic Albanians on both sides, not least because it obstructs business in smuggling centres, such as the municipality of Vitina in south-east Kosovo. Such frustration often translates into political instability. For the moment, much of the anger surrounding Kosovo's final status (on which little progress has been made) directly affects Belgrade rather than Skopje, but a further drift towards partition would have dangerous implications for Macedonia.

Background

Macedonia is a landlocked and mountainous country, with many rivers and deep valleys. Its 766km land boundary includes 151km shared with Albania, 148km with Bulgaria, 246km with Greece, and 221km with Serbia. Approximately 5,540km of its 8,684km of roads are paved. The country's ethnic composition is politically charged, with Macedonians (who are Slavs) constituting approximately 66% of the two-million population, and Albanians representing another 23% (the remainder is largely Turkish, Serb or Roma). The potential for ethnic violence remains high and is largely independent of the situation in Kosovo, while border disputes complicate the regional cooperation and facilitation of trade that might otherwise address the country's developmental issues. Several established trafficking routes run through Macedonia; a central European route crosses the Presevo-Valley section of the border north-east of Skopje in the direction of Belgrade, while an Italian route passes from the Tetovo area over to Prizen.[1]

From Skopje's perspective, the major border-related issues confronting Macedonia relate to continuing political and ethnic tensions, criminal or insurgent activity originating from across its borders, and its own lack of appropriate resources. From an EU perspective, the problem relates to the country's legacy and the Macedonian government's inability or unwillingness to deal with the country's troubling socio-economic realities, such as corruption.

As the Macedonian-Yugoslav border was not demarcated during Slobodan Milosevic's time, Macedonia never acquired the police and army experience or skills necessary for border management. Four months after Milosevic's fall in October 2000 however, the Skopje-Belgrade demarcation agreement was signed and Macedonian security forces began to patrol the border. This threatened the interests of organised crime in Kosovo and soon led to

Macedonia's forces clashing with protection units linked to smuggling chains running from Macedonia into Kosovo, Montenegro, Albania, and BiH, and on into Western Europe.[2] Indeed, the conflict of 2001 began when Macedonian troops tried to impose border controls in Tansuševci, a smuggling village south of Vitina on the border with Kosovo.

Insurgents and criminal gangs quickly took advantage of the security vacuum in the borderlands shared by Macedonia, Albania, Kosovo, and Serbia and Montenegro. Large tracts of Albanian-dominated areas were soon beyond state control and certain villages became notorious as transit points for illegal goods and as recruiting and training bases for Albanian extremists. The situation was exacerbated by high levels of illegal migration and human trafficking on the country's northern and eastern borders (much of it in transit to EU countries along the central European and Italian routes). In addition, Macedonia became an important trans-shipment point for heroin from South-west Asia and cocaine from Latin American. Meanwhile, drugs, weapons, tobacco and alcohol are widely smuggled.

Macedonia's borders are porous and unsafe, its border regions poor or corrupt, and the scale and intensity of armed confrontations on its borders are significant. NATO units are active and Macedonia's own border brigade is fully integrated into the military chain of command, reflecting the severity of the challenge. Border-security units from the under-resourced and ineffective regular police are only present at official border crossings, while the customs service is unarmed and reliant on the police for protection. Not surprisingly, much of the wider EU debate about border control is prompted by the insecure state of Macedonia's borders.

Strategic options

Macedonia's strategic options are limited. It can continue to place poorly trained military forces and ineffective police on its insecure borders, or it can gain international credibility by reforming its border system according to Schengen standards. Elements of both options are evident in practice, though Macedonia's formal objectives are dictated by the strategic priority of achieving EU membership; President Boris Trajkovski signed Macedonia's formal application to join the EU the day before his death. Macedonia is therefore in the process of reforming its system of border security according to the standards of the Schengen Catalogue.[3] The goal is to develop a specialised multipurpose police force through the IBM programme. The main instruments by which EU compatibility is to be achieved are EU SAAs for regulating relations and the financial instruments associated with the CARDS programme.

Macedonia's current strategy for border reform results from two potentially conflicting trends. The first is the dominant role of Macedonia's military in border security. Macedonian ministers argue that the main task of the army is to maintain the country's borders and ensure its territorial integrity – an expected stance given the circumstances. Regional security challenges may be shifting from military to criminal threats, but that boundary is blurred when the criminals concerned are heavily armed gangs. Responsibility for border security is consequently split between the conscript-based Border Brigade of the Ministry of Defence (MoD), responsible for surveillance of the land and water borders, and the MoI's Border Crossings Sector (BCS), responsible for formal border checkpoints. The BCS consists of police officers posted to border-crossing points on a rotational basis (there are approximately 6,000 uniformed officers in the police and 16 border-police stations). Though a level of cooperation does exist between the BCS and other agencies with an interest in border-related issues (such as customs, phytosanitary and health services), relations between the police and military are poor; police at border-crossing posts often have no information on the land borders running alongside the checkpoints.

The second trend relates to the international community's increasing interest in combating organised crime in the Balkans, rather than pursuing military-oriented peacekeeping operations. Echoing this shift, Prime Minister Crvenkovski argues that the main threat to Balkan stability is no longer armed conflict but criminality; Macedonia must therefore develop a police-based response.

Accordingly, Macedonia's priority remains national security ('the protection of the state border line'), but its goals now include developing coherent national border-management standards and transforming the existing surveillance regime based on the Army of the Republic of Macedonia (ARM) into a professional law-enforcement agency of specialised and dedicated border police. Many senior officers undoubtedly see the attainment of Schengen's standards as both conferring status and enabling personal gain. Vested interests also play a significant part in developments. Political infighting at the governmental level is intense, and senior officers are promoted, moved sideways, dismissed or retired (according to their political skills and connections) more frequently than in most EU forces.[4] Even so, political imperatives ensure that a more coordinated approach to border security is currently promoted. The strategy publicly endorsed is that of the EU's IBM.

The chosen strategy was formally approved in early 2002, and a working group was appointed to develop an appropriate approach. The subsequent project focused on four areas: strategy, IT, education and recruitment, and the drafting of amendments to existing legislation on defence and internal affairs. Attention then turned to building an institutional framework that could accommodate the requirements of key agencies with an interest in border security. These included: the MoI (sector for border crossings); the MoD (the army); the Ministry of Finance (Customs Office); the Ministry of Agriculture, Forestry and Water Management (Veterinary Directorate); the Ministry of Health (Sanitary and Public Health Inspectorate); the Ministry of Economy; the Ministry of Environment and Physical Planning; the Ministry of Foreign Affairs; and the Legislative Secretariat. This framework was to be underpinned by the technology of Global Information Systems (GIS). Control was then to be transferred from the MoD to the MoI, a move since facilitated by a series of workshops and study visits, and technical assistance from EU members and professional bodies. In early 2003, it was estimated that preparations for an IBM strategy and the creation of a dedicated border police would take six months; that the change and adaptation of legislation to support this process would also take six months, and that a similar time would be required to prepare an action plan to implement the changes.

Central to the strategy was a CARDS project intended to enhance the operational capacity of the new service within the existing organisational framework. This process would effectively fulfil immediate needs and develop the new organisational structure and operational capacities necessary for compliance with EU standards.[5] But even this preliminary step has proved an expensive undertaking. The cost of the four projects listed under the CARDS IBM programme was budgeted at €5m; €0.3m was allocated for developing IBM in 2002 and €0.5m for its implementation in 2003–04. The total sum was to cover the development of an appropriate strategy, the demarcation of the northern border, the construction of a data-communication infrastructure for border-crossing points, and the development of the required capacity for land-border management.

The timetable was reasonable, and police began replacing troops on Macedonia's border with Greece in May 2004. Six posts on the Greek border are to be fully transferred by November 2004, at which point the changeover will begin on the border with Bulgaria. The process will continue along the borders with Serbia (including Kosovo and Albania) throughout 2005, with November 2005 the target date for its completion.

Assessment

The current government broadly accepts the reforms promoted by international donors, but many of the associated programmes will take years to complete. In the meantime, the situation in Macedonia represents a real challenge to Schengen's standards and ideals, not least because any inability or failure on the part of the EU model to address Macedonia's border insecurity adequately would be politically and functionally significant. A positive experience would also go some way towards answering the broad question of whether or not EU-style guarding, as opposed to EU-style accountability, increases efficiency and effectiveness.

In particular, if EU-style border security is to have real meaning in the Macedonian context, it must not only acknowledge but also address factors subverting reform. This will require a degree of transparency, accountability and commonality, and an intolerance of corruption. However, the environment in which reform is to occur is one of political interference, organised crime, guns, entrenched corruption, social deprivation, ethnic tensions, and political and economic instability. Such factors affect the operational environment of guarding and the guards themselves, both as a group and as individuals.

The government's monopoly of armed force is challenged on the borders by radical nationalist groups such as the Albanian National Army (ANA), which has little popular credibility but claims to have active guerrilla forces in Kosovo and in the mainly Albanian

Presevo-Valley region of southern Serbia, as well as in Macedonia. The ANA pursues a pan-Albanian agenda and has close links with gangs operating in the former crisis areas of northern and western Macedonia, where cross-border smuggling is ubiquitous.[6] Such connections are important because organised crime is probably the single greatest threat to security and stability in Macedonia, and corruption the most insidious obstacle in the way of transferring Schengen's objectives and procedures. The gangs involved in organised crime skilfully exploit the weaknesses of members of the government and security forces, which in turn provide protection. The threat is intensified by the availability of guns. Access to guns is itself often directly linked to Macedonia's ethnic-Albanian insurgent groups, which not only run successful smuggling routes for weapons and cigarettes but also own criminal industries, such as production laboratories for amphetamines.

Corruption, meanwhile, affects every rank of the relevant security forces. It involves local policemen looking the other way and senior officials collecting extensive property portfolios and (in one notorious case) brothels. But it is not only officers who are open to bribery, for corruption especially at high levels of government, is endemic. It has evolved from passive exploitation to active coercion and in doing so has acquired the capacity not only to retard economic progress but also to feed organised crime and, in turn, political and communal instability. In effect, the state has come to function in important respects as a "racket", while the racketeers thrive in a culture of impunity.[7]

This climate has acute implications for the transferability of Schengen's ideals and for regional border management more generally, as Macedonia remains a source and a transit point for contraband and criminality.

Macedonia's system encourages autocratic administration, inefficiency and the politicisation of the security services, including those responsible for border security. Consequently, while current reforms represent an attempt to address many of the most accessible functional problems in Macedonia's border-security system, they fail to engage with the underlying social and political realities that determine its workings. Smuggling-interdiction capabilities, for example, remain limited, while the Border Brigade's doctrine is outdated, its tactical capabilities weak, and its ability to gather intelligence or conduct threat assessments is limited. Both the military and the police are inexperienced and inappropriately trained. There is no national security strategy as such.

Obstacles are present at every level and tend to relate to a fundamental lack of political will rather than inadequate resources. The MoI is seemingly unwilling or unable to cooperate with many of the external organisations offering training, and this despite continued funding from the EC. The EC disbursed half of the €3.3m allocated to police reform in the 2001 budget and, separately, it has through the EAR implemented a major programme for IBM involving customs as well as the proposed border police, which has cost some €14m over the past four years.

On the other hand, the international community's efforts are also limited. The EC/EAR may have considerable experience of central management, and the OSCE an impressive local presence, but the two do not cooperate and instead blame one another for setbacks. KFOR, meanwhile, cannot seal the border with Macedonia or solve the problems of the Serb or Albanian borders. Other initiatives are not wholly grounded in a desire for reform as such, but are instead political instruments for governments and intergovernmental organisations, which wish to generate positive publicity and be seen as adopting reformist policies that will bring about closer relations between Macedonia and the EU or NATO. Thus, the EU's 12-month Proxima police mission represents its political commitment to enhance regional stability, help Macedonia move closer towards EU integration, and support its government's efforts to fight the organised crime that could very well spill over into EU member states. Significantly, this contribution resulted from an invitation by Crvenkovski, then Macedonia's Prime Minister. While it is uncertain whether the initiative originated with Crvenkovski or with the EU's Secretary-General Javier Solana, both gained international approval as a result. In turn, Proxima received praise for its supervisory role in removing military personnel from border duties on Macedonia's border with Greece – also one of many measures (carried out under NATO's Membership Action Plan) aimed at preparing the country for NATO membership.

Proxima's stated budget stands at €15m, including start-up costs of €7.5m. Its aim is to help Macedonia's authorities develop their police forces to European and international standards, and its stated objectives include assisting the border police as part of the wider EU effort to promote IBM throughout the region. However, its 200 officers can only have a temporary and limited effect. Thirty officers are stationed at various border crossings, but their ability to change the 'bunker culture' of Macedonian police officers is questionable. Given Proxima's short lifespan, its promotion of EU-style community policing is likely to fail with Macedonian police forces stationed on the mountainous borders with Albania, Kosovo and Serbia and Montenegro, who would rather retain their camouflage uniforms, bullet-proof vests and Kalashnikovs.

Ohrid conference

Old- and new-style border management collide in Macedonia. In particular, the controversial role played by its military reflects a wider European contention regarding the appropriate balance between police and military roles in border management: the EU sees border management in Macedonia as an inherently civilian task and as part of its mandate, while NATO insists that its military-based approach is sometimes more appropriate given the circumstances. The dispute came to a head in May 2003 when NATO officials accused the EU of sabotaging a NATO-initiated conference on border security and management in Ohrid, a city on Macedonia's border with Albania.

The conference was called to develop a coherent approach to border security in the western Balkans. It addressed border management and anti-trafficking operations in Albania, Macedonia, and Serbia and Montenegro/Kosovo. It focused on the need for common political goals, objectives, principles and procedures, especially during transitional periods; that is, before the military withdraw and specialised police assume responsibility, or where military units are involved in protection or interdiction operations. Its aim was the eventual transfer of control to appropriate civilian authorities. Though Schengen standards clearly require border security to be the responsibility of the new border police, some NATO officials argue that Macedonia's northern border still requires a military presence; Kosovo's status is unresolved, armed extremists still enter the province, and ARM is currently involved in 'combat positions' in the crisis regions.[8]

Nonetheless, this apparent contradiction may not be so problematic. Some senior EU officers insist that both approaches may be appropriate according to context, while others promote the role of paramilitary units on the basis of France's use of gendarmerie. NATO, meanwhile, continues to provide advice on the military aspects of reforming and restructuring border security, which tend to involve bilateral and multilateral initiatives and encourage cooperation. Most guards accept the need for a rapid-reaction force and, regarding Macedonia, proposals for such a unit won considerable support within the international community. NATO was particularly keen, perhaps because it would help perpetuate its influence both in the country and more generally: the unit's personnel would be mainly military, with some police elements, and be under the control of the ARM in 'cooperation' with the police. NATO justifies the development of such a force as consistent with the overall framework for reforming the ARM – even though it would come at the expense of a civilian border police.

But the insistence by NATO (and by seconded Gendarmerie officers in EU organisations) on a military or paramilitary element is controversial. Macedonia has previously drawn international criticism over its use of paramilitary units, primarily the notoriously thuggish Lions, formed from police forces in 2002 by the then interior minister, Ljube Boskovski. The Lions were quickly disbanded, but only after diplomatic pressure from NATO and the EU, who presented the paramilitary group as an impediment to NATO membership. Significantly, when Prime Minister Ljubco Georgievski confirmed the Lions' disbandment in April 2002, he also stated that 1,200 of the original 7,000 Lions would be transformed into border-police units.[9]

The tension remains unresolved. The EU's objective of a specialised border police answerable to a ministry of the interior stands, but is seemingly applicable only in relatively benign circumstances. At the end of the Ohrid conference, delegates agreed that NATO would focus its support on the parts of the region where military units were temporarily involved in border control and interdiction, and that KFOR's involvement in such operations be closely coordinated with UNMIK, in accordance with agreed temporary operating procedures. NATO was to provide advice on the military aspects of reforming and restructuring border security through its civilian representative and liaison office in Skopje, and through its military representatives and HQs in Tirana and Skopje.

The picture presented by Macedonia's border management is thus mixed. Some progress is evident, but Macedonian authorities have yet to embark seriously on the reforms needed for effective border security. This step is needed to stem the trafficking that is of central concern to the EU. The continued involvement of NATO suggests limits to current EU guarding practices.

Albania

The capacity and desire of the Albanian state to develop effective border security, let alone adopt EU standards of management for its border police, are probably even lower than in Macedonia. Albania is situated on a traditional smuggling route, corruption is seemingly endemic, and EU standards of border management mean little in a society where there is no tradition of the rule of law, an underdeveloped notion of civil society, and an administrative culture developed for a repressive state. The ethnic-Albanian nationalists and criminal gangs working in Albania, Macedonia and Kosovo operate across borders extensively. Indeed, many Albanians regard the borders and boundaries established in the aftermath of Yugoslavia's fragmentation as a foreign – and illegitimate – imposition.

Background

Albania is a poverty-stricken state with 720km of land borders, including 282km shared with Greece, 151km with Macedonia, and 287km with Serbia and Montenegro. Its coastline stretches over some 362km. Only 2,900km of the 18,000km-road network are paved. Approximately 1700 border officers operate on behalf of a total population of 3.07m, of which 95% is Albanian. The terrain is mainly mountainous or hilly, with small plains along the coast. The main problems affecting Albania's land borders with Macedonia are trafficking in drugs and people, illegal immigration, and the smuggling of livestock.

Albanian provision for border security is, in theory, conventional.[10] Border security is understood as broadly as possible: it incorporates entry-and-exit control, prevention of illegal entry, combating alien smuggling, repatriation and issues of short-stays or transit visas. Border police, whose task is not shared with the army, staff all border checkpoints (though the specialised mobile groups replacing the old static units of the former Yugoslav regime are to be 'fused' with military units).

Authority for border security flows from the Ministry of Public Order, which delegates police duties to the State Police Directorate, and thence to the Central Border Police Directorate (which is part of the State Directorate), down to local border directorates.[11] Responsibility is shared between different ministries. The Ministries of Public Order and Local Governance share responsibility for immigration procedures with the Ministry for Foreign Affairs (which addresses migration issues), while the Ministry of Public Order (i.e. the Ministry of Interior) deals with transnational crime in cooperation with the Border Police Department, the criminal police department and the public-order police department. The law on the state police tasks the Central Directorate with controlling the state border and adherence to Albania's multinational border regimes and readmission agreements. All the relevant regulations are contained in the law on surveillance and control of the Republic of Albania.

The border-security budget forms 10% of the overall ministerial budget set by the General Directorate of the State Police. CARDS and the US provide most of the additional funding. Thus, US$200,000 was available for training in 2002-03, for example, while other funding for that year included US$525,000 for reconnaissance and preparation of the necessary border-security infrastructure, and US$5.9m for the completion of infrastructure requirements. The total US allocation of US$7,064,000 did not include funds for IT, which are provided by the US International Criminal Investigative Training Assistance Program (ICITAP).[12] Salary levels are set at approximately €400 per month for officers of the rank of major, and €175 for mid-level officers – but these figures are rarely reached in reality.

In practice, Albania's record is extremely poor. Attempts by Albania's government to address the problems of dishonest security services, high unemployment, decayed infrastructure, and entrenched criminality have been ineffective, while the activities of Albanian organised crime are notorious across Europe. Levels of trafficking in arms, contraband, and migrants are high, and Albania is a major trans-shipment country for illegal drugs from South-east Asia and Latin America destined for Western Europe. The implications for border security are serious.

Albanian border management is marked by inefficiency, corruption and lethargy. In reality, there is no separate, fixed, or formal border police. Indeed, the system barely functions. There are separate border-policing units inside the state police, and there is a specific recruitment policy, but border police do not have their own resources or career paths. The border police may have a fixed number of staff (about 1,680), but officers are rotated between the various state-police units and none are specialists. The majority of police officers lack training; others were trained under the old, isolationist and communist regime.

Schengen standards mean little to the untrained generalists, while the few with training from international projects cannot use their training because they are moved between units. Resources such as national and local databases in forged documentation do not exist. Add harsh weather and poverty to a deeply corrupt society and an almost total lack of resources and the realities of Albanian border management become only too clear, a reality reflected in the small, dark and broken-down premises found at many of Albania's border crossings.[13]

Strategic options

The past decade in Albania has been marked by political and economic instability, violence, and the rise of organised crime. Large sections of border-related legislation have been reformed in recent years, but not as part of a coherent strategy. There are however signs of change, as Albania's small Western-trained elite is increasingly concerned about its image abroad. In January 2004, for example, following the deaths of a number of illegal immigrants trying to reach Italy, the government introduced reforms to fight organised crime and reduce corruption amongst police and customs officials; this allowed it to claim that 2004 would be a decisive year in the fight against trafficking. Moreover, the government began talks with the EU on a SAA similar to those signed with Croatia and Macedonia. Nevertheless, EU member states remain concerned about the government's commitment to improve law enforcement and reduce corruption. Poor border security has been one of the greatest obstacles to Albanian membership of the EU (and also NATO).[14]

The strategic options available to Albania are limited but clear-cut. Albania wishes for better relations with the EU, and the latter can hardly afford to ignore Albania's non-existent border security. Indeed, given the numbers of illegal migrants transiting through Albania, the EU has an interest in aligning Albanian migration, border control and asylum policies with EU standards.

In March 2003, prompted by negative international publicity, the government formally accepted that it must develop a strategy for reform using the IBM framework. The ICMPD submitted a two-phase reform strategy for border control to the Ministry of Public Order; the 150-page report, *Upgrading the Border Guarding System of Albania along European Standard*, had been carried out by an international ICMPD-project team. The aim of the one-year project (financed by the EC under the High Level Working Group on Asylum and Migration, and the Netherlands) was to assess the state of Albania's border-control system, and to prepare a plan for improvement based on EU standards.

The report's plan involved the establishment of an International Border Control Task Force to support Albanian efforts at reform, and the preparation of a national action plan as part of the EU's CARDS programme. ICMPD also provided a project on migration controls and asylum policies intended to strengthen Albania's capacity to manage irregular and illegal flows of transit migrants. The project was financed by the EC, which has a budget for projects relating to the High Level Working Group on Asylum and Migration.

The reform strategy outlined in March 2003 required the Ministry of Public Order to report to the prime minister on the implementation of the first (analytical) phase of the project by January 2004, with a pilot implementation project to be completed by 2006. During the first phase of the project, an inter-ministerial group was assembled to address the coordination requirements of IBM for relevant agents and organisations, including customs, finance, transport, foreign affairs, the army, coast guard, anti-smuggling units of the Ministry of Finance, and foreign agencies such as the Italian *Guardia di Finanza*. Training and personnel development were also to be addressed, and an Academy of Public Order was established to provide knowledge on topics such as human-rights legislation, border-surveillance technology, IT and languages. Specialised units (to monitor maritime borders, for example) were to be created where appropriate.

These objectives complement the work of the EU, which focuses on helping Albania achieve a degree of compliance with Schengen standards. The EU's intention is to prevent illegal migration, strengthen trans-border cooperation, and establish effective surveillance and control using police methods. Other EU initiatives include the EU mission's police (which has been influential in developing Albania's strategy for border management), and a Customs Assistance Mission in Albania (CAM-A), which is helping Albania's customs improve its administrative capacities and functioning, notably through training, advice on customs procedures, the establishment of a human-resources management system, and the provision of equipment and support for computerisation. The EU also provides support intended to transform Albania's centralised economic and political system into a decentralised market economy and pluralistic society. In addition, the European Commission Police Assistance to Albania (ECPA-A) project includes assistance on topics such as border documents and procedures.

Other international agents include:
- IOM – migrant movement and the return and reintegration of trafficked women and children.
- OSCE Office for Democratic Institutions and Human Rights (ODIHR) – expanding regional and national anti-trafficking initiatives.
- Bilateral Italian-Albanian Mission in Albania (INTERFORZA).
- ICITAP – providing an IT-based information-management systems project.
- United States Agency for International Development (USAID) – working with Albania's Customs Office to increase state revenue and reduce corruption by establishing incentive programmes. USAID also provides training in customs methods and practices.

Indeed, so many bodies are now involved in the Albanian policing sector that the EU, in conjunction with the US, has established a consortium of 33 foreign and Albanian police agencies and NGOs in order to avoid duplication. In other words, Albania does not lack the technical assistance required to develop its strategy for border management.

Assessment

The Albanian government is keen to portray an image of effective border control and sustained efforts against organised crime, arms smuggling and uncontrolled migration. Nonetheless, real problems remain:

Geography Albania's coastal location and proximity to Italy ensure that illegal migration remains a major problem. The government has responded to EU pressure on people trafficking, but the drugs trade continues to flourish, something reflected by the building of smart new apartment blocks in smuggling centres such as the coastal town of Vlore. Additionally, the small size of the country makes maintaining secrecy a difficult task, and there is therefore little chance of gang members cooperating with the police; current plans for an ambitious witness-protection scheme are probably unrealistic.

Centralisation The government's attention is focused on Tirana, at the expense of Albania's border regions. The north is neglected and largely untouched by the political, economic and social progress evident elsewhere, with security remaining private and local.[15]

Guns The widespread proliferation of small arms makes guarding a dangerous business, particularly as large caches of arms and ammunition are hidden in isolated border regions.

Policing standards Contrary to the claims of some border officers, the public perception of the border police is generally negative and the functional standards of policing low. As the International Crisis Group (ICG) notes, the number of incidents on the Albanian-Macedonian border 'indicates inferior performance by border units generally known as the poor relations of the police'.[16] Even the police lack the incentives, skills and equipment necessary for effective control. Political interference, a lack of transparency or accountability, and a judiciary prone to corruption ensure that few of those arrested on borders are ever prosecuted.

Low policing standards are compounded by a gap between theory and practice, common across all levels of the border police. Thus, appropriate legislation exists but even senior officers struggle to identify the relevant laws and legislation. This is partly because officers working in border management rarely have knowledge of, let alone access to, the existing regulations. Further, while the border police are not part of the national police as such, it is improbable that they have avoided the factionalism, corruption and inefficiency that characterise Albania's other security forces.

Social realities: poverty, corruption and organised crime all obstruct effective policing.[17] Albania is probably Europe's poorest country; the per capita income is an estimated US$1,958, approximately 18% of the population have uninterrupted electricity supplies, and only one in six households has running water. The informal sector dominates in a society in which taxes are collected on a discretionary basis, and business is conducted in cash or kind.

The government has initiated a number of high-profile measures, such as *Operation Pune*, which was launched in 2002 and successfully targeted the Vlore-based gangs involved in ferrying illegal migrants and sex workers across the Adriatic to Italy. An international anti-trafficking centre has since been established in Vlore, but the highly profitable trade has continued; in January 2004, 21 illegal migrants died of exposure in a speedboat off the coast of Vlore. At best, government initiatives displace the smuggling operations, as targeted gangs simply move elsewhere. Indeed, with strong links with the Albanian diaspora in the EU, Kosovo, Turkey and the United States, Albania's traffickers have proven to be not only ruthless but also very flexible.[18]

Further, like its predecessor, the government of Fatos Nanos (which has been in power since 2002) pays little attention to the links between organised crime and guards, customs officials and politicians. Not only were corrupt police officers heavily involved in the trafficking targeted by *Operation Pune*, but the officers responsible for its success have since been dismissed as a result of restructuring initiated by a new minister of public order in early 2004. Corruption is unlikely to be addressed by a society in which all forms of business are conducted on the basis of personal connections. Given these factors, effective guarding is unlikely.

The obstacles to reform in Albania are serious. It could be argued that much has been achieved – most of it without outside intervention – in the decade since the collapse of the one-party state.

Indeed, the ICMPD believes that Albania's border management is 'in a transitional development process'.[19] What has not changed, however, is the political elite's inability or unwillingness to take corruption and illegal trafficking seriously. Similar considerations apply to the senior security officers, whose opportunities would be threatened by reform. Indeed, effective or efficient border security is probably not in the interests of either group. Accordingly, the implementation of reform strategies and the negotiations with the EU on a SAA have not resulted in genuine change.

It is noteworthy that Albania's border laws, like much of its legislation, now consist of an unenforceable mix of imported foreign standards.

Chapter 4

Regional Trends and Realities

Many of the obstacles impeding effective border security are common to all parts of South-east Europe. They include a lack of political will, a challenging terrain, lucrative smuggling routes, inadequate institutional capacity, corruption, and the low status of guards. But, as the four examples presented here show, significant differences also exist.

How and why neighbouring border services differ is best explained in terms of the political skills and vested interests of the senior officials and officers involved, social realities, and the geographical proximity of the countries concerned to the EU – the Schengen influence decreases with geographical distance.[1] While it is impossible to trace decision-making accurately, it seems likely that the developments discussed here are the result of officials and officers accommodating or subverting unavoidable political pressures, rather any desire for fundamental reform.

Each country is unique, yet common patterns of functional development are identifiable, and many of the assumptions underpinning regional explanations and practices of border security are shared. This is particularly noticeable amongst senior officers, many of whom know each other personally. To what extent, therefore, can a regional consensus be identified? To what extent has the significance of borders been blurred, or security become de-territorialised?

Shared assumptions

Most border forces in the region face similar problems. They seem to share a defensive culture comparable to that of the public police.

Each one of them aspires (publicly, at least) to meet the EU's principle of unified border security and to establish a dedicated force under the authority of an interior ministry, which is capable of cooperating at regional and international levels. Each country has the same formal core mission, and each shares a broad understanding of what border security entails. No doubt this owes as much to institutional interests as to Schengen standards, but it does ensure that a functional language exists amongst regional guards, which facilitates conversation even when the norms, techniques and procedures differ.

At the level of chief officers, this consensus is complemented by an acknowledgement of the importance of developing national strategies that can accommodate Schengen's requirements. There is agreement that border systems need to be based on politically appropriate concepts and definitions, and realistic threat analyses, and that the legal foundation of a system should be built on a core law that can be adapted or amended as needed.[2] This process is understood as an evolutionary and pragmatic matter, which must, however, take into consideration the relevant international, regional and domestic circumstances. Indeed, the need for increased regional cooperation is regarded by chief officers throughout the region as crucial for the development of effective and efficient border security and as a way forward for individual countries and for the region as a whole.

Schengen standards play a major role in the confidence-building that such cooperation would require. The development of common regional standards based on Schengen principles is accordingly emphasised by most officers, as are closer ties with Brussels and non-EU third countries, together with the exchange of border-related information, the creation of a regional risk-assessment system, joint operations along common borders, and a network of liaison officers. More generally, the stated priorities of many senior officers include operational issues such as the implementation of risk-assessment techniques, and greater cooperation regarding training. Existing technical and logistic constraints mean that the creation of technical-support units and shared databanks offered by some international donors are not, however, considered a priority.

This suggests that, barring major discontinuities or contingencies, regional cooperation is likely to remain at its current level for the immediate future – a continuity guaranteed by high levels of EU financial support. Meanwhile, the aims and objectives of the international community for the region remain as they were during the 2003 Ohrid conference: the establishment of open but controlled borders in accordance with EU standards and initiatives. Closer relations between the region and Europe are to be achieved by adherence to Schengen's standards and by guarding based on 'European' principles such as accountability and transparency – 'Schengen' and 'European' are seen as synonymous in the Balkans. The use of military units to exercise surveillance or interdiction is seen as temporary, and limited in scope and scale; responsibility is to be transferred to civil authorities as soon as possible. The means for achieving effective guarding are similarly uncontroversial; risk-assessment indicators, functional definitions, and techniques are to be developed alongside national strategies, action plans, and joint operating procedures and legal instruments. The EU, meanwhile, will support the development of IBM in each country, as well as regional cooperation mechanisms, with CARDS as the main instrument.

In this way, developments in the Balkans support the notion that the management of today's security challenges requires the integration of international, regional, national, and sectoral groups. All border forces in the Balkans regard regional initiatives (including joint-training centres, common standards in surveillance and control, and the exchange of information) as a priority. Most think that intra-regional ties, as well as those between the region and the EU and third countries, should be strengthened as a matter of urgency. In practice there are, of course, political limits to regional cooperation, even if these tend to be glossed over in public rhetoric. New-security challenges may threaten to overshadow the significance of borders in the wider European region, but security has yet to be de-territorialised in South-east Europe – witness the importance attached to border control in BiH and Macedonia.

Subversive spaces

The extent to which changes in the political rationale or meaning of border security have been prioritised over the functional transformation of the policing structures and institutions delivering it is, however, difficult to assess. To some extent, the search for an answer is unprofitable. It is impossible to disentangle the tight links between the EU's political project, its response to security threats that are not amenable to military solutions, the region's strong desire to be part of Europe, the inherent resilience of security organisations, the strength of vested interests, and the impact of local social-economic conditions. What is clear is that in recent years, the development of a regionally appropriate model of border security has been an EU priority, and pressure has been brought to bear on adjacent countries in South-east Europe (the term is politically significant) to adopt not only the EU's functional standards, but also its understanding of democratic management. Regional systems are expected to adhere to or reflect the precepts of the Schengen Catalogue and integrated border management. In addition, Schengen itself is attractive to the region's border guards as a means of enhancing their status; Schengen's complex rules must be implemented by a specialised, skilled and autonomous police force adhering to 'European' standards, rather than by the poor relations of a mistrusted public police.

Most senior officers accept the general principle that while border security ultimately serves national interests and is shaped by the geopolitical environment of border areas, Schengen standards represent an international benchmark. Many countries in the region confront challenges similar to those of EU applicant and candidate countries, and the EU's standards, as embodied within the Schengen acquis and Catalogue, are consequently seen as establishing criteria for appropriate functional standards against which regional border services can be measured. Even so, pronouncements by senior officers are often undermined by the actions of their juniors. Functional standards and normative values invariably adapt to local context, and the extent to which a strong consensual EU-style model of border security is developing across the region is less certain than the EU might wish.

The attractions of EU membership ensure that many of Schengen's criteria and procedures are acknowledged as desirable, but there is as yet little evidence to suggest that such standards have been absorbed. Further, it remains uncertain whether interventions designed to strengthen border control can make a real or lasting impact on the organised crime originating in or operating from South-east Europe. Whatever the case, the specific realities of South-east Europe's border regions mean that the embedding of EU-style accountable and transparent border management will be significantly more challenging than today's relatively straightforward transfer of technical or bureaucratic assistance. EU-inspired reforms have yet to be consolidated, and an appropriate balance between control and protection has yet to be found within the EU's framework.

It is not yet clear whether the EU's traditional approach of combining integration programmes with preventive measures, such as assistance in developing conventional border-security systems, will work. There is as yet little sign that the linkages between politics and corruption in the region have been loosened, or that development and exclusion problems in its border regions have been addressed. These issues must be tackled for the development of effective, let alone efficient, guarding. More generally, the formulation of cooperation goals and arrangements – and financial inducements – with countries such as Albania, BiH and Macedonia has worked so far, but contingencies (involving, perhaps, a charismatic politician promoting nationalism, or a dramatic upsurge in violence amongst Kosovo's frustrated and susceptible youths) could yet undermine the EU's preferred strategy.

In summary, recent political and social trends in South-east Europe provide evidence of how regional governments and security forces understand the predicaments posed by EU policies, but they also show how politicians and guards consistently contrive strategies that allow for the adaptation or evasion of political pressures. The trends identified in this paper show how such agents act in an unstable political landscape that lacks the strong political and social structures that support border-security systems within the EU. But they provide little evidence that either politicians or guards have attracted widespread legitimacy or popular acceptance. The next five years will pose stringent tests for the compatibility of EU ideals and norms, and the realities of the Balkan region.

Notes

Acknowledgements

The author thanks members of the International Border Security Advisory Board of the Geneva Centre for the Democratic Control of Armed Forces (DCAF), in whose company much of the research for this paper was conducted: Aare Evisalu, Arto Niemenkari, Andrus Öövel, Jürgen Reiman and Zoltan Szabo. The opinions expressed here are nonetheless those of the author alone.

Introduction

1 For an exception see Peter Andreas, *Border Games: Policing the U.S.-Mexico Divide* (Ithaca, NY: Cornell University Press, 2000), pp. 115-39; Andreas, 'Redrawing the Line: Borders and Security in the Twenty-First Century', *International Security*, vol. 28, no. 2, 2003, pp. 78-111.
2 Whether European guarding organisations should be referred to as a 'force' or a 'service' has more to do with politics than functional standards as such.
3 Working conditions (meals, lodgings, uniforms and personal equipment) and social guarantees (health care, housing, welfare) are not addressed here, though they are as important as regulatory

standards when it comes to determining how border management is delivered.

Chapter 1

1 Quoted in ICG, *Macedonia: No Room for Complacency*, Europe Report 149 (Skopje/Brussels: ICG, October 2003), p. 29; quoted by the Centre for SouthEast European Studies, www.csees.net/news_more.php3 ?nId=27412&cId=5.
2 See ICG, *Albania: State of the Nation*, Balkans Report 140 (Skopje/Brussels: ICG, March 2003). Compare Tim Judah, 'Montenegro fights criminal reputation', *BBC News*, 24 July 2003, www.bbc.co.uk; ICG, *A Marriage of Inconvenience: Montenegro*, Balkans Report 142 (Skopje/Brussels: ICG, May 2003).
3 For more recent statistics, see Peter Futo and Michael Jandl (eds), 2003 Year Book on Illegal Migration, Human Smuggling and Trafficking in Central and Eastern Europe: A Survey and Analysis of Border Management and Border Apprehension (Vienna: ICMPD, 2004).
4 Major omissions include the systematic analysis of comparative data, effectiveness, best practice,

and future trends. See
International Organisation for
Migration, *Migrant Trafficking and
Human Smuggling in Europe: A
review of the evidence with case stud-
ies from Hungary, Poland and
Ukraine* (Geneva: IOM, 2000), p.
79.

5   The ICG argues that the notion of
pan-Albanianism holds 'more
power as myth than as a practical
political agenda. That said, pan-
Albanianism is perceived by
many non-Albanians as a major
regional threat'. See ICG, *Pan-
Albanianism: How Big a Threat to
Balkan Stability?* Europe Report
153 (Skopje/Brussels: ICG,
February 2004), p. 31.

6   European Commission, *Bosnia and
Herzegovina: Country Strategy
Paper 2002-2006* (2002), p. 28.
europa.eu.int/comm/external_rel
ations/see/bosnie_herze/csp/02
_06_en.pdf

7   Andreas, *Border Games*, p. x.

8   'The Western Balkans and
European Integration', COM 285,
Brussels (2003), p. 2.

9   'Communication from the
Commission to the Council and
the European Parliament: The
Western Balkans and European
Integration', May 2003, p. 2,
europa.eu.int/comm/euro-
peaid/projects/cards/pdf/com-
munication.pdf.

10   See Christina Boswell, 'The
"external dimension" of EU
immigration and asylum policy',
International Affairs, vol. 79, no. 3,
2003, pp. 619–638.

11   Significantly, JHA represents the
principal area in which the EU's
overall policy of burden-sharing
operates. The notion of burden-
sharing was developed in
response to the influx of dis-
placed persons from the Balkans
prompted by conflict in the early
1990s.

12   See General Affairs & External
Relations Council, 'Countering
Terrorism: Council Conclusions',
8 December 2003,
europa.eu.int/comm/external_rel
ations/cfsp/intro/gac.htm#ter081
203

13   'Strange tales from Macedonia',
Jane's Foreign Report, 3 June 2004,
www.janes.com.

14   See European Community
CARDS Programme, 'Albania:
Country Strategy Paper 2002-
2006', 30 November 2001,
europa.eu.int/comm/external_rel
ations/see/albania/csp/02_06_en
.pdf

15   ibid., p. 36.

16   Boswell, 'The "external dimension"', p. 623.

17   ibid.

18   See Boswell, *European Migration
Policies in Flux: Changing Patterns
of Inclusion and Exclusion* (Oxford:
Oxford University Press, 2003).

19   EUROPOL, *2003 European Union
Organised Crime Report*
(Luxembourg: Office for Official
Publications of the European
Communities, 2003), p. 14,
www.europol.eu.int.

20   EU, *EU-Western Balkans Summit –
Declaration*, 21 June 2003,
europa.eu.int/comm/external_rel
ations/see/sum_06_03/decl.htm.

21   See Council of the European
Union, 'EU Action against
Organised Crime in the Western
Balkans', 14810/03, 2 December
2003, p. 1.
register.consilium.eu.int/pdf/en/
03/st14/st14810.en03.pdf

22   ibid., p. 2.

23   EC, CARDS *Assistance Programme
to the western Balkans: Regional
Strategy Paper* 2002–2006, p. 33,
europa.eu.int/comm/external_rel
ations/see/docs/cards/sp02_06.
pdf

24   ibid., p. 34.

25   ibid.

26   This section is based on Arto
Niemenkari, *EU/Schengen
Requirements for National Border
Security Systems*, DCAF Working
Paper 8, (Geneva: DCAF, 2002),
www.dcaf.ch/publications/Worki

ng_Papers/08.pdf.
27 Council of the European Union, General Secretariat DG H, *EU Schengen Catalogue. External Border Control, Removal and Readmission: Recommendations and Best Practices* (Brussels, 2002), p. 2.
28 See EU Press Release IP/02/661, 'Commission proposes integrated management of the EU's external borders to secure the area of freedom, security and justice', Brussels, 7 May 2002. europa.eu.int/rapid/pressRelease sAction.do?reference=IP/02/661 &format=HTML&aged=1&language=EN&guiLanguage=en
29 EC, *CARDS Assistance Programme*, p. 21.
30 ibid.
31 EU, 'CARDS Regional response strategy: Relation between CARDS national and regional support', www.ear.eu.int/agency/main/agency-a1a2c3n4.htm
32 *EU Schengen Catalogue*, p. 9. See also pp. 11–15.
33 For IBM see *Multi-annual indicative programme 2002–2004: CARDS Assistance Programme to the western Balkans*, which is annexed to the EC's Regional Strategy Paper 2000-2006. The main EU assistance programmes in Serbia and Montenegro, and Macedonia are managed by the EAR. The independent agency plays its part within the CARDS programme, which is in turn part of the SAp. See www.ear.eu.int/agency/agency.htm
34 See, for example, 'Financial, Organisational and Administrative Assessment of the BiH Police Forces and the State Border Service', 8 January 2004, www. icmpd.org
35 Irish Presidency of the European Union, 'Comprehensive Security: A Strategic Approach', EU Statement - ASRC 2004 Session 3, June 2004, www.osce.org/documents/sg/2004/06/3211_en.pdf.
36 US Department of State, 'U.S. Urges OSCE to Develop Coordinated Border Security Plan', 24 June 2004, usinfo.state.gov/is/Archive/2004/Jun/29-369807.html.
37 See Stability Pact for South Eastern Europe, Working Table 3: Migration, Asylum & Refugees, www.stabilitypact.org/marri.
38 'The Origins of the Task Force', Statement by Jonas Widgren (ICMPD) on behalf of the Border Guard Task Force of the Stability Pact, Bucharest 6 June 2002. www.icmpd.org/uploadimg/Bucharest%20Border%20Guard%20Task%20Force%20Stability%20Pact%20060602.pdf.
39 ibid.
40 'Athena' also refers to an EC decision of February 2004 whereby the Council agreed to establish a mechanism to administer the common costs of EU operations with military or defence implications. It effectively offers a permanent basis for the financing of operations. 'Berlin Plus' refers to a comprehensive package of agreements between NATO and EU, based on the conclusions of the NATO Washington Summit of 2003.
41 See International Crisis Group, *Collapse in Kosovo*, Europe Report 155 (Pristina/Belgrade/Brussels: ICG, April 2004), p. 41.
42 '"Complementarity" is a mysterious term used in EU development cooperation. Introduced in the Treaty of Maastricht, the concept ... is seldom clearly defined and the distinction between complementarity and cooperation remains blurred'. See J. Bossuyt, J. Carlsson, G. Laporte, and B. Oden, 'Improving the Complementarity of European Union Development Cooperation: From the Bottom Up', ECDPM Discussion Paper 4 (Maastricht: ECDPM, 1999), www.ecdpm.org.
43 Private discussion, Geneva, March 2003.

Chapter 2

1   The EU signed SAAs with Macedonia in April 2001, which came into force in April 2004.
2   This section is based on a series of personal communications and discussions with Jacques Klein, his advisers, SBS officers, and BiH officials, February 2002-March 2003. Klein was Principal Deputy High Representative with the Office of the High Representative in BiH from July 1997 until July 1999, when he became Special Representative. He held this post until 2003.
3   Even now, the security concept, especially at state level, is under-developed. International cooperation, for example, has to be channelled through a state-level agency.
4   See, for example, UNMIBH, *Borderline: An UNMIBH Bulletin on State Border Service Activities*, vol. 3, no. 14, 2002. The IMM-PACT initiative tackled the smuggling of people.
5   UNMIBH, *Borderline*, vol. 1, no. 3, 2000), p. 1
6   See, for example, the successful EU-financed programme provided by CAFAO (Customs and Fiscal Assistance Office to Bosnia and Herzegovina). As a result of CAFAO, customs revenue has tripled since 1996. BiH is now a single and uniform customs territory.
7   See, for example, Bosnia and Herzegovina Ministry of Security, 'National Action Plan for the fight against organised crime', 16 October 2003. formin.finland.fi/doc/fin/euasi-at/phare_twinn/Bosnia_ja_Herts egovina/Action_Plan.pdf
8   'The State Border Service is Making Great Results', *Tuzla Night Owl*, vol. 8, no. 321, 11 November 2003 www.tfeagle.army.mil.
9   Office for Auditing of the Financial Operations of the Institutions of BiH, Audit Reports Number 01-400-355/MG/02: *The Audit Report State Border Service of Bosnia and Herzegovina Year 2001* (Sarajevo, July 2002), www.revizi-ja.gov/ba/en/audit-rep/dgs01.asp#10
10 Judy Hylton, 'Security Sector Reform: BiH Federation Ministry of the Interior', *International Peacekeeping*, vol. 9, no. 1, 2002, p. 161.
11 UNMIBH-IPTF, Border Service Department, *Deployment of Bosnia and Herzegovina State Border Service Project Description* (version 1), February 2002, p. 16.
12 Nedim Dervisbegovic, 'Bosnia faces uphill task to meet tough EU terms', quoted in *NATO Enlargement Daily Brief*, 26 November 2003.
13 Much of the information used in this section was collected in Ljubljana, November 2002. It is supplemented by material from a series of discussions with senior Slovenian officers, January 2002-April 2003.
14 Personal communication, Ljubljana, November 2002.
15 Standard Summary Project Fiche, December 2001, p. 2, europa.eu.int/comm/enlarge-ment/fiche_projet/document/SI0 204.01%20Home%20Affairs.pdf
16 Until 2000, Albania, BiH and Macedonia were also beneficiaries of PHARE. In 2001, CARDS replaced this arrangement.

Chapter 3

1   See Neil Barnett, 'The criminal threat to stability in the Balkans', *Jane's Intelligence Review*, April 2002, p. 31.
2   See ICG, *Moving Macedonia Toward Self-Sufficiency: A New Security Approach for NATO and the EU*, Balkans Report 135 (Skopje/Brussels: ICG, November 2002).
3   The material used in this section is based on interviews and discussions in Helsinki, Kassel and

Geneva in April 2002, June 2002 and March 2003.

4   The political relationship between criminals and politicians raises disturbing questions. Compare European Stability Initiative (ESI), *Ahmeti's village: The Political Economy Of Interethnic Relations In Macedonia* (Skopje and Berlin: ESI, 2002), p. 17, www.esiweb.org/pdf/esi_document_id_36.pdf.

5   For details, see European Agency for Reconstruction, *FYR Macedonia Annual Programme 2003*, www.ear.eu.int/macedonia/main/fyrom-a1c2f3a4.htm.

6   See David Quin, Vladimir Jovanovski, Ana Petruseva, Naser Miftari, Artan Mustafa, Jeta Xharra, and Ilir Aliaj, *Armed to the Teeth: Disarming civilians in Albania, Kosovo and Macedonia means making them see guns are a threat to security, not a guarantee*, Investigative Report 470, November 2003, www.reliefweb.int/w/rwb.nsf/0/16b39ed35e51c2f2c1256dec004dd120?OpenDocument; ICG, *Pan-Albanianism*.

7   ICG, *Macedonia's Public Secret: How Corruption Drags the Country Down*, Balkans Report 133 (Brussels: ICG, August 2002), p. 1.

8   For an account of patrols on Macedonia's northern and western borders by US units in the late 1990s, see Bob Haskell, 'Guarding a Lesser-known Border: Macedonia', *Soldiers*, May 1998, pp. 20-23.

9   See Institute of War & Peace Reporting (IWPR) *Ohrid and Beyond: A cross-ethnic investigation into the Macedonian crisis* (London: IWPR, 2002).

10 The information in this section is based on interviews and discussions with Albanian and international officers and officials, April 2002–March 2003.

11 The Coast Guard is incorporated within the Ministry of Defence.

12 For more information see International Criminal Investigative Training Assistance Program (ICITAP), 'ICITAP Project Overviews: Albania', www.usdoj.gov/criminal/icitap/albania.html

13 A simple comparison between the resources available to Albanian border guards and those of BiH has implications for the mobilisation of technologies across jurisdictions. Most Albanian controllers have little more than a pen, a notebook and an old telephone; working radios and vehicles are rare (in late 2002, the border police had approximately 90 hand-held radios and ten vehicles, none of which had been maintained). The SBS, meanwhile, received in the summer of 2003 a package from the German Border Police including 18 surveillance vehicles, 21 minibuses, computer equipment, passport-inspection devices, photocopiers, and a training programme. Albania's situation also raises questions about the appropriateness of the assistance offered by some donors. The sophisticated technological solution offered by ICITAP is a case in point. Intent on improving the Albanian National Police's ability to combat illegal trafficking, ICITAP provides a 'Total Information Management System (TIMS) initiative that will provide the ANP with the technology to connect all border entry/exit posts through a computer network and thereby enhance its ability to control the country's borders'. See 'ICITAP Project Overviews: Albania', usdoj.gov/criminal/icitap/albania.html.

14 Kerin Hope, 'Albania: Crackdown follows EU pressures', *Financial Times*, 18 December 2002, www.ft.com.

15 See ICG, Albania: *State of the Nation 2003*, Balkans Report 140 (Skopje/Brussels: ICG, March 2003), p. 10.

[16] ibid., p. 13.

[17] ibid., pp. 7-11.

[18] For the linkage between the diaspora, politics and crime see ICG, *Pan-Albanianism*, pp. 25-27.

[19] Personal communication, Geneva, March 2003.

Chapter 4

[1] The relative importance of internal and external factors is difficult to assess. Some, notably Jan Zielonka, suggests that it is 'difficult to maintain that external pressures are more effective in shaping democratic procedures (constitutions, electoral rules, etc.) than democratic processes (such as a shared understanding of the rules of the democratic game, common norms and values, and habits of reciprocity and compromise)' .See Jan Zielonka, 'Conclusions: Foreign Made Democracy', in Jan Zielonka and Alex Pravda (eds), *Democratic Consolidation in Eastern Europe: International and Transnational Factors* (Oxford: Oxford University Press, 2001), p. 531.

[2] This section is based on material presented by regional representatives at three DCAF workshops, Geneva, January–March 2003.

For Product Safety Concerns and Information please contact our EU
representative GPSR@taylorandfrancis.com
Taylor & Francis Verlag GmbH, Kaufingerstraße 24, 80331 München, Germany

www.ingramcontent.com/pod-product-compliance
Ingram Content Group UK Ltd.
Pitfield, Milton Keynes, MK11 3LW, UK
UKHW021437080625
459435UK00011B/285